Acc

 MW00529481

Raymond's Room
Ending the Segregation of People with Disabilities

"*Raymond's Room* will create the same kind of outrage as the blatant racial segregation of the 1950s or the discrimination against women in the early part of the 20th century."
— *Paul Wehman, Ph.D.*
Professor and Director, Rehabilitation
Research and Training Center on Workplace Supports,
Virginia Commonwealth University

"If confession is good for the soul, then *Raymond's Room* has, indeed, been good for me...should be required reading for all who are committed to dismantling the disability industrial complex...Thank you, Dale, for telling the truth."
— *Ann Turnbull, Ed.D., Professor, Special Education,*
University of Kansas; Co-Director, Beach Center on Disability,
Council for Exceptional Children,
Burton Blatt Humanitarian Award, 2006

"*Raymond's Room* describes a reality we might like to think is in the past. Yet, it is the present reality for people with disabilities and for society. This book reminds many of this reality and tells a history that most do not know. Dale has provided a call to action that should be heard by people inside and outside disability circles."
— *David Mank, Ph.D.*
Director, Indiana Institute on Disability and Community,
Indiana University

"...a must-read for anyone who has ever wondered how the field got to where it is and whether there are better ways to connect people to work and to community life."
— *Richard Luecking, Ph.D.*
President, TransCen, Inc., Maryland

"*Raymond's Room* needs to be required reading...It speaks the unspeakable truth that all of us as members of our communities and society at large, aided by the 'disability industrial complex' Dale describes that we've created, daily commit unconscionable illegal acts and crimes disguised as 'helping the handicapped.'"
— *David Hammis, M.B.E.*
Senior Partner, Griffin-Hammis Associates, Ohio

"...in essence people with disabilities are still 'locked' away from the mainstream of society...I hope that this book will be used for staff training to open the eyes of future leaders in the disability field."
— *Katherine Inge, Ph.D., O.T.R.*
Director of Instructional Technology, Rehabilitation Research and Training Center on Workplace Supports, Virginia Commonwealth University

"This book lays out why segregation occurred and still occurs and the negative impact that it has on the lives of individuals. This is a thoughtful book that provides insight...I wish that I had this book to read early in my professional career, as it would have helped me to understand the larger picture of service delivery systems."
— *Keith Storey, Ph.D.*
Professor of Education and Special Education Program Chair Touro University, California

"For far too long, all of us in the system have been willing to accept the small gains experienced by folks with disabilities as acceptable. *Raymond's Room* kicks the door of acceptability back open. This book will cause all of us to rethink our roles in building full community opportunities for all people. ...puts reality right back in our faces. It raises consciousness, ignites passions and brings the spirit back into our work. If you have forgotten the story that got you interested in disability issues, this book will be your awakening."

— Al Condeluci, Ph.D.
Executive Director, UCP of Pittsburgh

"This is why we need *Raymond's Room* by Dale DiLeo: to remind us that people with disabilities still live lives controlled by others...and to shake us from thinking that what Dale writes is the past, when in fact, for many, many people, it is the present. Get this book and read it."

— Cary Griffin, M.A.
Senior Partner, Griffin-Hammis Associates, Montana

"Wow! Dale DiLeo has written a compelling book that is long overdue. A must-read for EVERYONE!"

— Vicky Davidson, M.Ed.
Developmental Disabilities Program Manager
Missouri Planning Council for Developmental Disabilities

"...an excellent resource for self-advocates, families, and professionals. One of the most significant publications I have read in my thirty-one years of working in the field."

— J. B. Black, Ed.D.
Training and Research Manager, State Disability Agency

"This is a must-read for anyone involved in supporting people with significant disabilities, whether they be family members, paid staff, policy makers, neighbors, or advocates."
— *Bob Niemiec*
Past-President, APSE - The Network on Employment

"*Raymond's Room* awakens our conscience. It challenges our beliefs and progress in this field and suggests greater attention to the most basic of human needs: love, respect, caring, and hope."
— *Richard M. Balser, M.A., C.R.C.*
Maine Medical Center
Chief Outpatient Services, Department of Psychiatry
Director, Department of Vocational Services

"Dale's message is loud and clear. It is time to end the 'us and them' mentality in every dimension of our society. Living, working, playing and participating in life to the fullest is the right of every citizen, regardless of disability!"
— *Nancy J. Hanisch, M.S.*
Florida APSE: The Network on Employment

"This is a one-of-a-kind book. Dale artfully offers readers the chance to experience 'cathartic cleansing' from their personal experience of Raymond's room, without excusing us from doing what is right and just. Be prepared to look deep within your core values. This book is as much a call to mind as it is a call to rally and action. Chipping away a little at a time at the wall that segregates people with disabilities has not been successful and is no longer acceptable. Read the book to learn why and what we must do."
— *Ernesto Sanchez*
Regional Manager, Advocacy Inc., San Antonio, Texas

Raymond's Room

Ending the Segregation of People with Disabilities

By Dale DiLeo

Training Resource Network, Inc. ● St. Augustine, Florida

This work is based on the author's actual experiences in the disability field, and no individuals described are intended as the basis for case studies. Steps have been taken to disguise the identities of individuals who may have been used in composites and embellishments for desired communicative effect. Thus, any resemblance between persons represented here and real persons is coincidental.

First Edition

This publication is sold with the understanding that the publisher is not engaged in rendering legal, financial, medical, or other such services. If legal advice or other such expert assistance is required, a competent professional in the appropriate field should be sought. All brand and product names are trademarks or registered trademarks of their respective companies.

Published by Training Resource Network, Inc., PO Box 439, St. Augustine, FL 32085-0439. You may order direct from the publisher for $15.00 US plus $5.00 shipping by calling 800-280-7010 or visiting our website at www.trninc.com or www.raymondsroom.com.

Printed in the United States of America on acid-free paper.
ISBN-13: 978-1-883302-55-9
ISBN-10: 1-883302-55-2

Library of Congress Cataloging-in-Publication Data

DiLeo, Dale, 1953-
    Raymond's room : ending the segregation of people with disabilities /
by Dale DiLeo. --1st ed.
        p. cm.
    Includes bibliographical references and index.
        ISBN-13: 978-1-883302-55-9 (alk. paper)
        1. DiLeo, Dale, date. 2. People with disabilities--Institutional care--United States. 3. People with disabilities--Abuse of--United States. 4. People with disabilities--Services for--United States. 5. Social integration--United States. 6. Special education teachers--United States--Biography. I. Title.
HV1553.D527 2007
362.4'045--dc22

For my girls: Dawn and Letty

TABLE OF CONTENTS

π—0

ACKNOWLEDGEMENTS

There have been so many supportive people in my career and during the writing of this book. Thanks especially to Dawn Langton, my editor (and wife and partner of twenty-seven years), Laura Lee Smith, who edited my drafts and helped guide my writing process and our book promotion, and Chris Smith, who skillfully designed the cover. Thanks to my friends in New England where I first learned what was possible in serving people with disabilities: Janis King, Denise Sullivan, Kathleen Spencer, Nathan Gilfenbaum, Dave Yeiter, Gordon Allen, Susan Covert, Ruby Moore, and Ric Crowley. Also, thank you to the many colleagues in the disability field who not only tolerated my tirades, but often joined me as I would rant about injustice: Dave Hagner, Karen Flippo, David Mank, Tammara Geary, Celane McWhorter, Derrick Dufresne, Rich and Debra Luecking, Ann Noll, Frank Greenburg, J.B. Black, Pat Rogan, and Bob and Anastasia Lawhead. Thanks to Cary Griffin for his assistance with photos, and to the Center on Human Policy, Syracuse University, for granting the right to reprint photos from *Christmas in Purgatory*. I owe a debt also to three colleagues and friends with whom I had the privilege to work closely and who have since passed away: Rebecca McDonald, Herb Lovett, and Dick Lepore – there is a hole where your passion used to be. And thank you for your friendship, "casserolers" of St. Augustine. Most of all, I want to express my gratitude to those people with disabilities who have continually taught me that lots of things can happen to you in life, but how you choose to live makes all the difference.

●

"... segregation distorts the soul and damages the personality. It gives the segregator a false sense of superiority and the segregated a false sense of inferiority. Segregation... is not only politically, economically, and sociologically unsound, it is morally wrong and awful."

— Martin Luther King

π—0

P R E F A C E

Writing a book of memoirs always seemed to me to be a task for people who have lived lives of high achievement, were in the eye of the public, or had amazing events happen to them. None of these things are true of me. So an explanation is due you, the reader, for why I have chosen to write this book. I have spent much of my career working with people who have disabilities. This is not a very high-profile profession. It is respected primarily because people believe it is such a self-sacrifice to do this type of work. But my work has provided me with invaluable lessons about life. It has taught me about how we view people with differences, how we value each other, and how society responds to those who have needs. I think we have failed people who have disabilities in many regards.

I started out my career in this field while I was finishing my undergraduate degree at the University of Delaware. In my first job in the field, I was part of the night staff at a small private residential school for autistic children. Over the years since, I was a teacher's aid, a teacher, a head teacher, and program director. I also served as an executive director for two agencies. I ran day programs, oversaw group homes, and directed case management. I eventually earned a master's degree, as well as certification as a special education teacher.

Ultimately, my path as a professional dramatically changed my outlook about services for those with disabilities. I entered the field as a clinician and teacher, analyzing, charting, and modifying behavior. I believed very specialized settings were the best way to serve people with disabilities. In short, I tried to fix people.

Now I am a consultant, and have been for the last twenty years. I now believe that we can best support people when we help them to learn about their options and to live the lives of their choosing. I now see how most specialized settings are *segregated* settings, places that create far more obstacles then they remove. Finally, I have learned to get to know and understand people before I give them professional advice.

In the thirty-plus years that I have worked in the disability field, I have been both a participant and an observer in the lives of people with disabilities. What has been remarkable to me in all that time is what many people have accomplished in their lives, not just despite their disabilities, but despite the attitudes and expectations of many of those around them.

I guess there really is a "time for every purpose." I started writing this book at least fifteen years ago. Then, about two months ago, during a break in my schedule, I came across my manuscript, a pitiful few pages stapled together. Successful writers have always said the same thing: Don't write unless you have some truth to reveal. I reread my work, threw it out, and started over. This time, the bulk of the manuscript just poured out over the course of weeks – I think it would have been merely days if I did not have so much other work to do. I guess it just took a while before I understood myself what it was I had to say.

The anecdotes about people that I tell here come from many facets of my work. I have modified names, places, and situations to protect privacy, anonymity, and confidentiality. Most of these events I experienced personally, although I have sometimes added fictionalized dialogue for purposes of readability. Lest anyone believe that these tales are exaggerations, however, I recommend you go and talk to anyone who works in this field. You will hear echoes of what I have described here, including comedy, drama, tragedy, and everything in between.

In short, this book is a like a stew. It is a memoir of my career, combined with the lessons I have learned, with criticism and a little advice thrown in for seasoning. It wanders through events much as I wandered through my career. I try to talk a little about what I learned from each person and each situation. As you read, you may recognize some things from your own life. And maybe these flashes of recognition will teach you something, as they did for me.

FOREWORD

The horror of the past collides with the dismal reality of present day thinking in Dale DiLeo's engaging memoir about his coming of age in the disability profession. DiLeo invites us into his life and mind, as well as into the one-room prison that represents the systemic exclusion and isolation perpetuated by the present matrix of services for people with severe disabilities. *Raymond's Room* provides poignant real-life vignettes that examine how the disabilities services system can unintentionally exacerbate a person's existing life challenges.

That DiLeo is qualified to provide such accounts is beyond question. We recall listening to him for the first time many years ago and being awed by his commitment, humor, and passion. Over the last three decades he has witnessed and contributed to improvements in the lives of some of the most vulnerable people within our society. To us, he has been a stalwart colleague and trusted friend.

The issues explored within the pages of *Raymond's Room* reflect the author's journey through learning and applying best practice within a system that remains resistant to change. DiLeo characterizes this lack of progress as being due to the "disability industrial complex" (DIC), an insidious bureaucracy of traditionalists funded by methods that serve the status quo. The DIC is based on the historical assumption that this disenfranchised group of people is best served by specialists within isolated settings, an assumption that is not only immoral but also ineffective, costly, and most certainly illegal.

The cost benefit to taxpayers of services resulting in integrated work and housing has been demonstrated continuously over the past twenty-five years. The present widespread professional allegiance to segregated services should have ended in 1990 with the passage of the Americans with Disabilities Act (ADA). That this segregation continues to occur following clarification of the ADA's "most integrated setting" standard through the Supreme Court's 1999 Olmstead Decision is criminal.

This is the largest group in the world facing systemic discrimination in all areas of life and represents the "last bastion of lawful segregation in employment and housing." The way in which we in the United States have forced people with severe disabilities to live is a national disgrace. In the past we didn't have the understanding and technology to fully realize the invaluable contributions citizens with significant disabilities are able to make. For several decades, we have proven in communities all over the country what people are capable of achieving. And yet, the statistics in DiLeo's book speak for themselves. We quite simply are not using what we know and what we have learned to support the vast majority of individuals. DiLeo vividly illustrates this gap between what we know and what we do. People with severe disabilities and their families will be all too familiar with many of the experiences described within these pages.

As the aging parents of a ten-year-old son, our concerns are escalating in a time of blocked progress and dwindling resources within human services. It is our hope that DiLeo's provocative insights into a system gone awry will ignite a revolution in people with disabilities, their families, and friends. It is up to each of us to take the inspiration generated by *Raymond's Room* and change the world for those we love.

–Bob, Anastasia, and Jessie Lawhead

Bob, Jessie, and Anastasia Lawhead

●

When you open a sealed jar containing hundreds of flies, only one or two will leave immediately. The others will continue to circle around the jar aimlessly, as if their world was still constrained.

Why don't they leave?

They have predicated their current world from a specific reality from their past, despite the fact that it no longer applies.

People do this, too. Psychologists even have a label for it (of course). It is called *premature cognitive commitment*. It describes a fixation to a reality without considering new information.

We are much too like those flies.

π—0

INTRODUCTION

I once worked in a place where the rules were the rules, and all of us staff were very young. It was in 1975, very early in my career, and the place was a residential facility for children with autism. Most of the residents were challenging. Some were aggressive; others would hurt themselves.

Management decided that three residents in particular must live in a secure room at night. The room was a small space, about eight by ten feet, not much bigger than a walk-in closet. It was largely taken up with two sets of bunk beds. There was no other furniture. There was also no "overnight staff," just the owners of the facility, who had a bedroom and lived in the residence. In truth, I doubted that they looked in on any of the residents in this "home" very often. So to secure the room of the three most challenging residents, the outside of the door was locked, closed with an eye-hook and latch.

From the outside. Overnight.

Was this a breach of every safeguard, fire policy, and human rights policy I now know? Of course. But because we were all right out of college and had no real training in the realities of this business, we accepted the explanation we were given by those in charge – that this was for the residents' own protection: the only solution for people so severely disturbed.

But it gets worse. This room had a radiator controlled by a thermostat in the hall. In summer it was stifling on its own. But in winter, overnight, with the door closed and the heat on, that room would get really hot. More troubling still, since the door was locked, there was a portable toilet inside. Combine the heat with the smell, and the room was simply unbearable. Opening that door each morning was difficult, and one could only imagine what spending the night inside was like.

This was called Raymond's Room.

Raymond was the room's most permanent resident. Other students were assigned there from time to time, but Raymond never moved from his room. He was the resident who couldn't be trusted, and he had been in this room so long it was now named after him.

Many things happened overnight in that locked room. I know because I often discovered things in the morning when I came on my shift. I once spent a day with a resident cleaning the feces Raymond had smeared on all the walls and beds. When I went home after work, I threw out the clothes I wore that day and took a shower that lasted an hour. How anyone could sleep in there, I do not know. How I could *let* anyone sleep in there haunts me today.

There are far fewer places today physically like Raymond's Room. But the kinds of lives people like Raymond must live actually have changed little. The way in which we have separated people with severe disabilities from the world, and continue to do so, is a national disgrace.

People have a tendency to divide the world into simple categories, preferably two: black and white, them and us. Regarding disability, people believe they are either in the world of the healthy or the world of "the disabled." The healthy have compassion for those in that other world, but view that kind of life as a place apart, and don't have any sense of real affinity for those in it.

I once read a performance review of a disability staff person that captures this feeling. It said, "Ms. Covington has a personality that blends in well when working with people, as well as with her clients with disabilities." These individuals, apparently, do not qualify as just plain people.

Yet, disability, as expressed in U.S. law, is a "natural part of the human experience."[1] To some extent, we all are healthy, and we all have our "disabilities." Precious few of us are completely functional, either in body or mind. It is all a matter of degree. But more importantly, it is also all a matter of outlook and perception.

People with significant disabilities are society's "hidden citizens." They are the "them" to most of "us." Though often out of everyday view, their numbers are surprisingly large. For example, various studies in the U.S. approximate the number of people with developmental disabilities, including intellectual disabilities, as 1.9 million for people eighteen years or older[2] to between 3.2 and 4.5 million if you include all ages.[3] The number of individuals with severe psychiatric disorders in the U.S. can be estimated by those in the category "mental disorders other than mental retardation" who receive Supplemental Security Income (SSI) and Social Security Disability Insurance (SSDI), the two federal programs that financially support individuals with disabilities. This was 2.9 million people in 2004.[4]

No matter which study is more accurate, there is undeniably a significant number of people with severe disabilities, the great majority of whom are living lives separate from the rest of "us" (those of us without disabilities). If not institutionalized, they are largely segregated in facilities or houses, many of which are not welcomed in our neighborhoods.

Those that are in "our" communities are not really a part of our communities. They may live and attend day programs in our neighborhoods, but they remain institutionalized in spirit and thought.

As children, they do not go to school where our children go to school. They attend completely different schools, or "they" must go to separate "special" areas or classes.

As adults, they generally do not work where "we" work. They attend training programs that have largely failed at getting them into the workforce. When they earn money, they make wages no one could live on. Some are legally paid less than a penny per hour for doing work few of us would want to do.

They are the last minority group in which legal segregation for housing and employment is still routinely provided. And their lives are controlled by one of the last publicly funded monopolies in America today.

Yet, the know-how to support even the most disabled of our citizens has grown tremendously. We have learned how to help people with severe disabilities get real jobs for decent pay, live in their own homes with support, and socialize and control learned behaviors that present difficulties. We also have seen profound changes in accepted philosophy and ethics about how we should view and help people with disabilities.

But there is a serious disconnect between our new-found technology and philosophies and what is happening in practice. Most of the program directors that I have met, let alone direct service staff, have little time to read journals or new books. They might go to a conference and hear new ideas, but a lot of them have expressed to me that they believe the speakers don't realize the day-to-day challenges they face. Many then conclude that their agencies cannot make the kinds of sweeping changes that are proposed.

Part of the problem with changing a system is that it is hard for those in it day after day to see what might be beyond their daily concerns. There is an old Yiddish saying that reminds us that to a worm in a horseradish, the whole world is a horseradish.

We construct our reality based on the information we have at a beginning point in time and a belief in what it means, regardless of whether it is no longer true. During a visit to London, an acquaintance told me of a story that appeared in the *London Times* several years ago. It seems a man heard an owl nesting in his garden. Each night, he would go outside and hoot to the owl. After several nights, much to the man's satisfaction, the owl began hooting back. This exchange went on for months. One day, the man's wife was talking to her neighbor, who told her that her husband had also been going out every night to hoot to an owl. After a moment of consideration, they realized that, in fact, both husbands had spent many months hooting to each other! I think the constant hooting at non-existent owls aptly describes our current disability system: it has not made adjustments based on new information.

Slowly, the segregation of people with disabilities is being challenged. But by and large this advocacy is not coming out of the leadership of the disability service system that serves these individuals. The challenge is coming from courageous advocates, some of them professionals, many of them people with disabilities and their families. They want something better; they are beginning to realize that it is in reach, and the system is not giving it to them, despite our own laws.

The preface to the Americans with Disabilities Act states:

"...society has tended to isolate and segregate individuals with disabilities, and, despite some improvements, such forms of discrimination against individuals with disabilities continue to be a serious and pervasive social problem." [5]

It is not just society that has isolated people with disabilities, it is the disability service system itself. I believe we already hold many of the answers to this challenge, but we have lacked the will to put them in place. History should be a guidepost, not a hitching post.

This book talks frankly about the continuing failure of the system that provides services to people with significant disabilities, from institutions to so-called community-based programs, including sheltered workshops, day treatment programs, and group homes. But it also discusses the challenges the system is up against – how our society perceives those who have a disability, and what these perceptions translate into.

And finally, it talks about the promise of the future – a time when people with all kinds of disabilities will live among "us," work with "us," and attend "our" schools, churches, and social events. This will be a time when people with disabilities will not feel a need to hide, disguise, or deny their disability. In fact, depending on the disability, many disability advocates promote "disability pride." It is equality that is needed, respect for all, and a level playing field, not sameness. Ultimately, we will all be part of the "us," and our differences acknowledged.

I never forgot Raymond's Room. As my career progressed, it came to stand for everything that was wrong with the way we provide disability services. As this book describes, I have struggled to advocate and fight for change in lots of disability arenas since; some of my efforts have led to small changes, and some, I like to think, have had a bigger impact.

But I have considered more than once whether I have stayed in this low-paying, challenging field to somehow atone for what I did not do as a very naïve young man –

– unlock Raymond's Room.

CHAPTER ONE

One Toothbrush: Institutional Life

"Four decades of work to improve the living condition of children with disabilities has taught us one major lesson – there is no such thing as a good institution."
– Gunnar Dybwad

I still remember the feeling of anticipation I had, waking up in the early morning darkness. It was my first day on a new job in my chosen career. Although still in my senior year at the University of Delaware, I had finished most of the credits I needed for college. This was going to be an amazing job. I was going to be a "special teacher" for students with autism at a local residential school in southern Delaware.

After three-and-a-half years at college, nothing had grabbed me, until junior year, when I volunteered as a psychology intern. One facet of my internship involved visiting a young man with autism. He seemed unusual in every way, from how he talked to the way he rocked back and forth. I didn't understand him, and never really got to know him, but I found autism itself to be fascinating. This was in 1974, way before the current explosion of autism diagnoses, books, and public discussion.

I felt lucky to have a position teaching youngsters with autism. I arrived at school early. "School" was actually an immaculate, three-story farmhouse where about thirty children and adolescents slept and ate. There were six bedrooms, three baths, and a room for eating. There was a small outbuilding where classes were held. All this was set on farmland surrounded by a white split rail fence. It was quite a peaceful setting.

As the other teachers arrived, they gathered in a small room. Al, a friendly, kind, broad-shouldered man, had been at the school for three years. He was the head teacher.

"Hey, look who's here, bright and early, ready to go," he said to me.

I just smiled.

"Well, follow me and I'll show you the morning routine."

Al explained that I would wake up the residential students and help them dress, wash up, and eat breakfast. Then I would take "my group" of five children to a classroom, where I would be responsible for their lessons. I followed Al as he went up the stairs to the children's bedrooms. The bedrooms were filled with bunk beds, boys separated from girls. The curtains were dark blue, with Disney characters smiling down. But that wasn't the first thing I noticed; it was the stench that hit my nose. A couple of the bedrooms had portable toilets in them, and the smell was sickening.

One by one, Al and the other three teachers began to wake up the children. Some were already awake, rocking back and forth. Some had gotten out of bed and were wandering about.

"Wake up, Bobbie. C'mon Mike!" Al led the teachers through a get-em-up, get-em-ready routine that was army-like in its efficiency: shake each child awake, lead them to a toilet, dress them, then bring them upstairs to the dining room. There, the children each got a glass of milk for breakfast. That was it. I was shocked.

"How could a kid go to school on just a glass of milk?" I asked Al.

"Well, the director feels that this way the children will be motivated to earn food treats during classes. That's how we train. The kids work, and if they do a good job in their morning session, they get some marshmallows."

"Marshmallows?"

"Yeah. We'll explain how the sessions work when we get to class," Al replied.

I knew that whatever the explanation, there was nothing that would make it acceptable to withhold a child's breakfast.

"OK everyone, let's get everyone to take a turn in the bathroom and then brush their teeth," Al called.

I went over to observe. Al was brushing every child's teeth, using the same tired-looking, yellow toothbrush. After the third child, I could watch no more. I walked outside to the schoolhouse, sat in a small child's chair, and felt a tear come down my face. This was not what I expected at all.

In a meeting with the director later that week, I spoke out about that toothbrush and the lack of breakfast. I was tentative in doing so, because the professionals in charge were older, more experienced, and, in the case of the director, very intimidating. But to my surprise, my timid complaint led to a real change. Maybe in my innocence I shamed the owner, but within a short time, all the students had their own "bathroom buckets," filled with their personal hygiene items. This was still no way to live, but it was certainly an improvement.

This simple change began my personal commitment to improve the lives of people with disabilities. I admit this began rather quietly early in my career. I didn't challenge much except the most grievous situations. I now know that there were many more things I should have protested. But I continued to question things more and more over the years. I now try to challenge the status quo in human services wherever I see that it fails people.

Ultimately, my path as a professional changed my outlook about services dramatically. By 1984, after ten years working with people with disabilities, I had grown completely disenchanted with traditional human service programs. I was now trying to help more people with severe disabilities access community settings in more typical ways, instead of through formal, segregated disability programs. I was speaking out much more loudly now.

This chapter focuses on institutions, but much of what I discuss here also applies to the chapters that follow on community services. What I eventually learned too well is that very bad things can happen to people in the name of treatment and protection, especially in segregated settings. This is not a new or revolutionary finding. As a reminder, one need only remember the exposés in the 1960s and 1970s about institutions like Willowbrook in Staten Island, New York.

A History of Neglect

Conditions in Willowbrook were first brought to the public's attention when New York Senator Robert Kennedy made an unannounced visit there and to the Rome State School in 1965. The media widely covered his reaction to the institutions' filth, odors, overcrowding, and inadequate care. This shocked many and led to a public outcry. The response from state officials came quickly. They bitterly complained that the senator took only a whirlwind tour and was offering a misleading picture, reacting only to the worst of what he had seen.

In response, a professor at Boston University, Burton Blatt, visited five other institutions in the northeast US. In exchange for a promise not to identify the schools, he arranged for tours of their back wards. On each tour, an accompanying professional photographer friend took pictures using a hidden camera attached to his belt. The photographic journal he produced, *Christmas in Purgatory*, horrified many. The book opens with the line: "There is a hell on earth, and in America there is a special inferno."

I am looking through my old copy of *Christmas in Purgatory* once again as I write this, and the images are just as striking as when I first looked at it many years ago. It graphically shows poorly dressed and semi-nude people, rows of beds in sparse, dirty halls. The barrenness is stark. Said Blatt,

> *"Although our pictures could not even begin to capture the total and overwhelming horror we saw, smelled, and felt, they represent a side of America that has rarely been shown to the general public and is little understood by most of us."* [6]

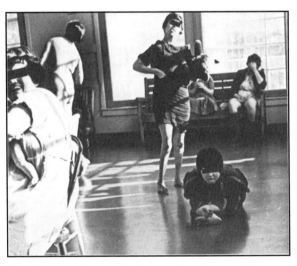

Photo from *Christmas in Purgatory* courtesy Center on Human Policy, Syracuse University

Photo from *Christmas in Purgatory* courtesy
Center on Human Policy, Syracuse University

This was followed by more Willowbrook revelations sev-
en years later, first by newspaper stories chronicling conditions, and then by a series of televised reports from an eager
young New York television reporter named Geraldo Rivera.
Using a stolen key for access, his film crew documented still
squalid conditions in understaffed wards. Almost 6,000 New
York residents with disabilities lived in Willowbrook during
the 1950s and 1960s. At the time, it was the largest facility of
its kind in the nation. The resulting public outrage lead to a
series of changes that still affect the disability system today.
Rivera, many years later, said, "...the lovely exterior belied a
monstrous world hidden behind windowless walls and locked
doors." [7]

Postcard of the Willowbrook facility

Willowbrook closed in 1987. Since then there have been significant efforts to improve conditions in state-run institutions. But are poor living situations in places like Willowbrook the real problem? Is cleaning them up the solution? I believe the conditions we often find in institutions are only a symptom of the real issue – the isolation, segregation, and congregation of people with disabilities. It is the structure of institutional design that lends itself not only to deplorable conditions, but to needlessly limiting the quality of life for the residents that live there.

Institutional Life Continues Today

I worked in two different, relatively small-scale residential facilities for people with disabilities. I think both would still qualify as what we today term "institutions." And they were as clean as could be, with most of the staff as kind as anyone I know. But looking back, I think the people who lived there lived in an intolerable hell. And I think no one, but no one, on the basis of a disability, should ever have to live in such a place again.

The numbers of people with developmental disabilities living in big institutions has fortunately gone down steadily over the past thirty years. From its peak in the 1960s, when close to 200,000 people were institutionalized, it declined to about 40,000 in 2004, with projections of less than 20,000 by 2016.[8] According to recent research, of the approximately 500,000 persons in the U.S. with developmental disabilities who are in "out-of-home residential placements":

- 21% are in facilities with 16 or more persons,
- 11% are in facilities with 7 -15 persons, and
- 68% are in 1-6 persons settings, with about half of those typically in places called "group homes."

The cost to support these different settings is eye-opening. For example, the larger state-operated institutions cost, on average, $146,000 per person per year in 2004. Think of what that could buy a family annually who wished to support an institutionalized person in their home! In settings of six or less persons, supported living/personal assistance cost only $21,000. Use of a funding stream for small community homes called the Medicaid Home and Community Based Waiver averaged $38,000 per year per person.[9]

Big-scale solutions to housing people with disabilities seem inevitably to cost more. But, again, the costs are only one small part of this troubling picture. One of the quickest routes to dehumanization is to group people based on their perceived deficits in order to "treat" them. And dehumanization begets compromises in lifestyles. People cease to be treated as real people.

It is easy to see how this approach to disability services has evolved. It is based on the medical model of service. People with a medical condition go to a specialized center, such as cardiology or oncology, to obtain the services of people who are experts in their problem.

But having a developmental disability is not the same as having a medical condition, although certainly some disabilities include medical conditions. A developmental disability is generally a life-long condition that often requires planning, services, and support in a variety of areas for the individual to experience a quality life. Obtaining services should not occur on an inpatient basis. Services for people with disabilities often entail life-encompassing supports, including housing, vocational, and daily living assistance.

A Life Apart

In many states, the courts have intervened over services provided in institutions. They have mandated that residents of institutions receive better access to "community life." This is so the individuals will be more "integrated." Of course, with so many people and limited vehicles and staff, the only way to do this is for the institutional staff to take people out as a group.

Sign posted outside state group homes warning community members not to venture near. Photo courtesy Cary Griffin

Group outings for people with disabilities into the community (it sounds like some kind of safari into the wild) are not something that happens just in institutions. They are a common practice in the adult service system in local communities. But if you've ever seen a group of people with developmental disabilities or mental illness out in the community, you know that "integration" is not likely, by some magic, to happen for them. Unfortunately, the group is often such a spectacle that even basic conversation with someone from the community is unlikely.

Ernesto was a staff person I knew at a state institution for people with developmental disabilities. He was a sensitive person who really tried to help the people he cared for live better lives. Over time he was promoted to ward supervisor. As part of a movement in the disability field toward greater community integration, Ernesto started a "community access" program.

The first trip was scheduled. Arrangements were made with a local bowling alley for the institution to use half the lanes for the following Tuesday. The community day came. Twenty-two residents of Ward Three, Ernesto, and three other staff members boarded a rented school bus. The residents rode wide-eyed to the bowling alley. For some of these people, it was their first trip outside the ward for a long time.

Twenty-five people got off the bus. Not Ollie, however, one of the institution's residents. His feet seemed to have concrete shoes. Ollie decided he wanted nothing to do with bowling, the community, or anything else outside the bus that day. He was staying put.

Those residents who did leave the bus were not used to being out of the ward. Albert and Casey got off the bus, spied the Dunkin' Donuts sign across the street, and took off in pursuit of the holy land. Ella got off, saw the traffic, and tried to crawl under the bus.

"Ella, get out from under the bus. Ron, get Ella out of there. Albert, Casey, please come back! Everyone line up! Allison, if you don't stop pinching Michael, you will stay on the bus with Ollie..." Ernesto was a bundle of nerves. After everyone finally made it inside, the second act ensued. Bowling balls and bowling shoes seemed to be everywhere. "Bob," pleaded Ernesto, "one ball at a time. Albert, come back. Mary, you can't walk down to the pins..." And so it went. The five bowlers from the community who were in the alley left after ten minutes. Ernesto was exhausted. When he returned to the institution, he dutifully filled out each person's report. Under the heading "community integration," he checked off "accomplished."

But what was really accomplished? Sure, these institutional residents got to see a part of life they had never seen. That in and of itself was probably worthwhile. But it now seems like a small grain of sand in the beach of life. Visiting to see what life looks like isn't sufficient, however nice it may seem. *Being* in life is what is important.

Over and over again, I have found that disability services have taken people out of their families, communities, and lives, much like a vacuum cleaner sucking up unwanted debris. The reason given is generally that this is "for your own benefit." And to rectify this obvious displacement, the system tries to visit what was left behind, in order for people to "experience integration." It is a poor simulation of life.

Institutional Design: Convenience Trumps Individual Preference

Certainly not all institutions these days are alike. Many have made efforts to spruce up surroundings. Still, people who are made to live in institutions must find it incredibly boring. From my experience, an institutional ward, no matter how it is decorated, offers little to interest a person. They are still sterile places, usually barren. They are filled with endless tile, dormitory furniture, and bland walls. And, when they are decorated, the decor is not a personal expression of any individual who lives there. It is as if you are out to sea in a small boat. The scenery looks pretty much the same every day. Where else is there to go?

Stark walls and an open closet for residents' jackets. Photo courtesy Cary Griffin

As I noted, institutions are not always places filled with lots of people. I once went to visit a young man named Dirk. I had agreed to volunteer as Dirk's court-appointed guardian, and I wanted to visit him in his "home," which was a relatively new building tucked away in rural Florida. I don't recall the number of people living there, but it wasn't that large. I figured a visit was the best way we could get to know each other, and I could also learn where and how he lived. (Unfortunately, making personal visits is often not the case with guardians and their wards. Because so many guardians are state-paid "public guardians" who have large numbers of people to keep track of, many do not really get to know their wards very well.)

Dirk lived in a "residence" that I could best describe as sterile. He shared a room with three other boys. He had few possessions. But the thing that really struck me was the design of his room. It had a window, with blinds, that looked out to a hallway. When I looked at the window, I thought something just wasn't quite right. Then it dawned on me – the blinds were on the outside of the window, in the hallway! This is classic institutional thinking. The purpose of the blinds was not for the boys' privacy, but for the staff's convenience to look in at them.

The bathroom had the same approach. The toilets were lined up against one wall, but they were not enclosed in individual stalls. The idea of personal privacy just didn't enter into the architectural planning. When I asked why, the answer I got was always the same: it was for the residents' own safety. Some were self-injurious; they would hurt themselves and had to be monitored. It seemed to me then, and still does now, that one could pay attention to people without making their every private action open to public scrutiny.

From an institutional bathroom. There are no dividers between the stalls. This was so staff could tend to three people at a time when they were marched in in the morning and all made to toilet at the same time. Organizational convenience trumped privacy. Photo courtesy Cary Griffin

I think people make these types of design decisions because they are boxed into a system that is too confining in
the first place. A lack of privacy is considered a necessary
compromise because of the institutional design, not because
it is the only way to help monitor and prevent self-injury. I
remember the staff of one facility I worked at buying living
room furnishings for a common room. They selected ugly
couches and chairs because they offered two things – ease of
cleaning and urine-resistance.

The Deinstitutionalization Movement

There is a word for moving people out of institutions
– "deinstitutionalization." When applied to people, it describes the process of finding them a place to live and spend
their days in their home community with all the needed supports. Applied to a system, it implies the gradual closing of
the institution as more and more people move out. But there
is another way to view deinstitutionalization, and that is to
move people out of services that are stuck in institutionalized thinking. Institutionalized thinking is, at its core, based
on the need for people who have a disability to be segregated.
Woody Allen once said 80% of success in life is showing up.
Segregated people with disabilities aren't allowed to show up.

Opposition to ending such segregation continues fierce-
ly, whether it is in defense of sheltered workshops, residential facilities, or institutions. As far as I can tell, the opposing
voices are not the people with disabilities themselves. They
are either some of the families who have made what must
have been an agonizing decision to have their family member
attend such a place, or the disability professionals who often
direct, consult with, or work in these facilities. For instance,
Bernard Rimland, an early researcher in autism and an advocate of institutionalization, writes:

> *"It's time to replace the deinstitutionalization move-*
> *ment with a 'common sense' movement that acknowledg-*
> *es the diversity of our children and the need for institu-*
> *tions and group homes, and other options as well...Many*
> *medically fragile or behaviorally disordered clients are*
> *a danger to themselves and others when placed in group*
> *homes where staff training is inadequate, supervision is*
> *lax, and local doctors are ignorant about developmental*
> *disabilities. Such individuals need other options, including*
> *institutions...Farms and ranches should be encouraged,*
> *as they may readily combine the best features of institu-*
> *tions...with the best features of group homes (home-like*
> *settings)."* [10]

I couldn't disagree more. I, too, have deep problems with how many community services are run. But I think institutional advocates have set up a false choice. People don't need institutions because some group homes are bad or offer inadequate support. We absolutely know how to properly support people with medical or behavioral challenges without resorting to institutional placement.

But You Are Taking Away The Right to Choose!

Another common argument is that by taking away the institution, we are removing "choice" from families who wish to have that option. I agree that this is true. But I think it is about time that this particular choice is finally removed. This is because, with what we know today about how to support people in community settings where all of us belong, it is plain wrong to offer such an option. But more importantly, it is wrong because we should not use taxpayer funds to segregate people who have done nothing wrong, whatever challenges they pose.

Government makes decisions all the time about what choices it will provide its citizens and what it will pay for. Most everyone agrees that we have a moral obligation to support our citizens with disabilities, but there is nothing implicit in that belief about doing so through an expensive, tax-payer-funded model that takes people out of society and puts them in a simulated society "for their own good."

I also think this applies to sheltered workshops. In this case, we are spending public funds for people with disabilities to work in segregated settings that offer abysmal outcomes in terms of wages and eventual job placement. If this were the only option we could figure out, that would be one thing. But it isn't. There are new alternatives that allow us to help people with very challenging disabilities work in real jobs, in integrated settings, making more money and receiving less pubic benefits while paying more taxes.

Notice the phrase "home-like setting" that Rimland used. You will hear a lot of that kind of phrasing in disability services. "This residence is home-like." "Our workshop is just like a real business."

Photo from *Christmas in Purgatory* courtesy
Center on Human Policy, Syracuse University

But people with disabilities shouldn't have to live in home-like settings, or work in pretend work environments. People – all people – need real homes and real jobs. At a recent training, I asked the people there whether their agencies still ran sheltered workshops. Nearly all raised their hands. I then asked why people with disabilities were still attending segregated work programs. One man spoke up and said, "Well, it is still a *viable option* for our individuals, because of their disability."

Viable option? What does this mean? I looked up "viable" and it was defined as: "the state of being usable, practical, or healthy." In other words, the viability was due to what his agency believed was practical. Not only is there no evidence to support this that I know of, but its morality is questionable.

A Personal Commitment to
Not Make "Better Institutions"

I worked in New Hampshire from 1977 to 1991. My years there happened to intersect with a remarkable time in the state's disability system. By the year I left, New Hampshire became the first state in the country to close its only public institution for people with developmental disabilities, the Laconia State School.

This was a result of a 1978 class-action lawsuit, *Garrity v. Gallen*. In 1981, Judge Shane Devine issued a court order for the state to deliver services in the "least restrictive environment." This ultimately led to the creation of a community-based system of services and supports – a local "area agency" system that focused on local communities supporting local people.[11]

I was offered the position of superintendent of the Laconia State School during the years of downsizing by the director of the state agency that oversaw all state services for people with disabilities. It was a tempting offer. But ultimately, I found I was more drawn to the building of a community system than I was to the dismantling of an obsolete institutional system. It is an approach that stays with me today, regardless of whatever "obsolete" model we talk about.

In fact, I made a decision many years ago to no longer consult with or train institutional staff. This was not because I thought they were bad people, or that it was a waste of time. I decided that with my own limited resources and time, I was philosophically opposed to trying to reform places that ultimately needed to close. I would rather invest in communities where people with disabilities should live, work, and play.

I mean no disrespect to those who work in institutions; in fact I have great admiration for them. Many of these people strongly agree that the residents of the institutions should leave. And yes, closing a facility takes time, and in the meantime, services and supports must be provided. While I understand this, I still do not feel I am the right person to provide training in institutional settings. For example, an institution once asked me to conduct a seminar on how to do "person-centered life planning." This is a process I will explore later, developed for community life and conducted by each individual and the community members who have a personal, caring relationship with the person. I have a difficult time believing it is worthwhile to take these principles and help people apply them from an institutional environment.

In my polite declining of the training offer, I was told I was arrogant for choosing where my services could have the most impact. I hope not. This was a personal decision after many years of soul searching. I do think we should all be willing to go anywhere, anytime, to discuss ending segregation or the reasons we should help people with disabilities be included in community life. I have never said that I would not go into an institution in order to get people out – or to talk about why it should ultimately close.

I guess my message was that I would not go to an institution to help make a better institution. I suppose there is a bit of arrogance in that, but it is a choice I have made based on where I think I can do the most good.

Some people also believe they can instead make the institution a "kinder, more gentle" place instead of moving people out into their communities. What I believe is that it is a fallacy to think that you can reform an institution to become a quality community-based service. You might improve it in a variety of ways, but you can't really say that a large, rather unnatural, segregated setting can get closer to being a true community of diverse people. An elephant is still an elephant, however you try to dress it up. You don't apply new technology or bring in more "non-disabled people" for integration to happen, for instance. You get people out. You try to close the doors. Otherwise you become part of the process that is sustaining the institution, even if it is a little bit better.

Yes, there are still people with disabilities who live in institutions that will not close anytime soon and whose lives are important, and this concerns me. I don't think we can forget about these people. Of course conditions must improve for them immediately while they still live there. But I think we should make it our first priority to redouble our efforts to get them out into quality community settings, rather than trying to make their segregated lives just a little bit better. So, I have made the choice over the years to invest my time and resources to build a better community for them to come to, not a better institution. Forgive the pun, but you just can't teach an old dogma new tricks.

I realize not everyone agrees with this position. But I have had many experiences of going in to a segregated program with good intentions of helping it to change, only to be disappointed by what evolved. If you are a disability professional reading this, I hope you realize, as I did, that each of us must choose his or her own path, but we should be open to other's experiences.

Since 1991, several other states, including Alaska, Maine, New Mexico, Rhode Island, Vermont, and West Virginia, have followed the route of closing their state institutions for people with developmental disabilities. More states are close to realizing a non-institutional system. Over the thirty years of my career, the numbers of people living in institutions has declined steadily. It is my hope that I will live to see the day when we end a shameful era of the large-scale removal of people from society based on their disabilities – a day when no one lives in a state-run institution in this country. I believe it is only a matter of time. Once, upon returning from a shopping trip, Ronnie, an individual newly released from an institution, was uncharacteristically exuberant. A staff person asked me, "Why is Ronnie so excited?" I thought about it and said, "I think he has had a near-life experience."

But here's the rub. Imagine you are a person with a disability leaving institutional life for the community and community-delivered support. Leaving the institution for the community system doesn't mean you will always be welcomed as a part of the community. Instead, you still might find yourself in a smaller but still segregated program doing something of little interest to you, surrounded by other people who share your label. Institutional thinking has followed you to your community, just on a smaller scale.

Now you are stuck in the Disability Industrial Complex.

CHAPTER TWO

Labeling and the Disability Industrial Complex

"Strangers on the street are moved to comment: 'I admire you for being out; most people would give up...' They think they know everything there is to know, just by looking at me. That's how stereotypes work."
–Harriet McBryde Johnson

In 1977, after three years of teaching at the school for children with autism in Delaware, I gave notice and took a year off from human services. It was a break I sorely needed after the regimen of institutionalized training and care I had been giving. I had been playing guitar part-time in a local folk-rock band, and we were doing well. I wanted to see what would happen if I focused on music full-time. At the same time, everyone in the band agreed we should move to New England, a location friendlier to our type of music. So along with my girlfriend and future wife Dawn, my bandmates and I ended up living in New Hampshire.

It was soon apparent that the challenges of making a living in music, along with the constant travel, were going to require more than most of us in the band were able to give. I soon was looking for a job once again in my field. I ending up accepting a position in a local public school district as a teacher's aide. This was a very short-term job experience, because I soon landed a teaching position at another residential facility for children with autism. But my public school experience was very memorable for me because of one accomplishment – my work with Jack.

"Tank-you, Mr. D."

"Dale," said Ms. Jameson, "This is David. You will be working with him as his one-on-one aide."

Ms. Jameson was the special education teacher in charge of a class of eight students with varying degrees of intellectual disabilities. Because I had some knowledge of sign language, which David was learning to better be able to communicate, my job was to tutor David in reading in the classroom.

"Hi David," I said.

"And this is the rest of the class: Jack, Ronnie, Rachel, Terry, Carl, Joan, and Steve."

I smiled at everyone. They all looked at me warily, except Jack. He just looked away.

In a classroom of eight children with developmental disabilities, Jack was the shyest. He was ten and was labeled as having mental retardation. He work thick glasses and had the sweetest smile. He rarely spoke and was hard to understand. I took to him immediately.

David was a fun kid, and we made good progress, but I soon noticed Jack keeping a close watch on what David and I were doing. When I asked the teacher about Jack, I learned that there were few expectations for him to read. He was considered not ready, too disabled. I asked if I could work with him whenever time permitted. After much discussion with the teacher, my request was finally approved.

I sat down with Jack and told him we were going to play a kind of game. I was going to show him things and he was going to tell me what they were. We started by using objects. I placed in front of him a pencil, an eraser, and a small ruler.

I would say "pencil" and he would point to the correct item. We did this with several different objects, always using three options at a time. This proved easy enough for him. I soon started introducing little cards into the mix with pictures on them, like an apple or a horse.

Jack thought this game was fun. I made it as exciting as I could, showing amazement and surprise whenever he answered correctly, making him laugh. We soon moved into a more challenging area, and I started slipping in a card that had printed on it a word.

I would introduce it by saying, "This card has a word – apple." Then I would mix up the three items.

"Now, find APPLE."

Jack pointed to the card.

"Good, now what is this word called?"

"Apple."

"That's right! You are amazing! OK, now I will trick you. Where is...HORSE?"

Jack smirked. Then, with a growing confidence, he pointed at the other card with the word "horse" printed on it.

"What, are you sure?"

Jack looked up at me expectantly, then nodded.

"Well," I said, "you're right!"

He grinned, which to me seemed to be the biggest joy expressed that I have ever seen from anyone. And on we went, a new word each day. I was now using a simple instructional approach, presenting three whole words at a time. I used this whole sight word approach instead of phonics and sound rules, which I think would have confused him. I managed the process so that he would succeed nearly all of the time, and we celebrated each victory, which made him light up.

By the end of a month, Jack was reading sentences and had a reading vocabulary of more than thirty words. I was as astonished as everyone else. One day he read a whole paragraph out loud in front of the principal. His whole demeanor had changed; he was so proud. On my last day in the classroom, he did something I had never seen him do before. He came over to me and gave me a solid hug around my legs, then looked up at me, smiled and said, "Tank-you, Mr. D."

That moment has stayed with me all my life. In fact, in this field, these are the kinds of moments you live for. I wondered why what I did for Jack couldn't have been done in a regular classroom, where Jack could have become friends with other kids in his age group.

As much as I loved the kids with whom I was working, my aide position did not pay me much more than minimum wage. Financially, this was the poorest Dawn and I had ever been. Our income was barely enough to pay the rent and buy groceries. And when the cold came on that first winter in New England, it was probably due only to the fact that our parents had given us decent coats for Christmas that we even survived. I starting interviewing for other jobs, and soon got an offer to be a teacher once again for kids with autism, something I now had a lot of experience in.

Out of Institutions for Good

I left the teacher's aide position in 1978 and accepted the job at the autism program. This required another relocation, to northern New Hampshire. The new program focused on more of what I had done before – trying to stop kids with autism from acting "inappropriately," while teaching them various academic skills that I could scarcely imagine them using in adulthood. I spent several years as teacher, "master teacher," and then acting director for the program at this school. But it was never a good fit. Like my first job, this place also approached kids in an institutionalized fashion.

We collected lots of data and utilized "behavior management programs" in which staff gave highly structured responses to each infraction of a behavioral rule. Instead of being on a farm, this school was on a hilltop, surrounded by open country. This seems to often be a feature of institutional thinking – finding safe places out of town with lots of room, whether to protect the residents of the institution or the community from the residents is unclear.

I spent three years there and managed to get my master's degree while working. During this time, Dawn and I were married, and before long, we both felt we needed a change of scenery. Fortunately, as New Hampshire began to move people out of its institution at this time, I was offered another job in southern New Hampshire heading up a new program for adults with disabilities. This was perfect, as Dawn was pursing her master's degree at a graduate school in the same area. So we again relocated.

I, of course, had no idea at this time that the frequent job changes I was having was quite a normal phenomenon in human services. Turnover in the disability field has always been high, and continues to be today, mostly due to the low wages and high demands.

My new job put me in a whole new world of community services for adults with disabilities. This was a system that I eventually came to realize was a complex web of programs. They offered much promise, but were very difficult to access, let alone respond to the individual hopes and desires of a person with a disability.

I had left the world of institutions, only to enter the Disability Industrial Complex.

The Disability Industrial Complex

In 1961, after the massive military build-up through World War II and afterwards, President Dwight Eisenhower warned the nation of the undue influence of a military industrial complex. His words aptly describe what happens when the power to control events becomes concentrated in a mutual relationship between parties that support each other's existence and goals. Eisenhower warned that it is exceedingly challenging to balance a mega-system whose primary goal is to perpetuate itself, rather than serve the real needs of its government. In part, Eisenhower said:

> "...we must guard against the acquisition of unwarranted influence, whether sought or unsought, by the military industrial complex. The potential for the disastrous rise of misplaced power exists and will persist.
>
> We must never let the weight of this combination endanger our liberties or democratic processes. We should take nothing for granted. Only an alert and knowledgeable citizenry can compel the proper meshing of the huge industrial and military machinery of defense with our peaceful methods and goals, so that security and liberty may prosper together.
>
> Akin to, and largely responsible for the sweeping changes in our industrial-military posture, has been the technological revolution during recent decades. In this revolution, research has become central; it also becomes more formalized, complex, and costly. A steadily increasing share is conducted for, by, or at the direction of, the federal government." [12]

Today there exists another industrial complex apart from the massive military one. It, too, grows more formalized, complex, and costly. It is the service system for people with various disabilities – the Disability Industrial Complex

(DIC). (I honestly don't remember the origin of this term. I remember attending a conference many years ago and having a conversation with people about how powerful the disability system was and how hard it was to get it to change. The DIC term came up then, and I have used it ever since.)

The comparison to the military industrial complex is striking. The DIC is also vast and complicated, often self-serving. Unbeknownst to most of the public, it is a huge industry, aided by government-sponsored grants and often costly technology. As I have said, I have been a part of this industry for many years, as are many of my colleagues in the disability field. I do not make my case for radical change from the outside looking in. I do this from the perspective of a paid professional on the inside, from providing direct service to being an executive director or a consultant for various programs in the system.

Being Part of the Past Shouldn't Prevent the Future

I have not been removed from most of the problems I talk about in this book. I have not spent my life as an academic, studying policy or doing research. I had a hand in delivering or managing many programs at one time or another – programs that I now criticize. I think that those of us who were a part of a system, providing in good faith those services that are now obsolete, need not be criticized for what we did. At the time, we hopefully were providing what was considered then as a "best practice."

It is those who refuse to change or be open to new ideas with whom I now take issue. Even though they are confronted with better ideas, new technologies, and new approaches that have been confirmed by research to provide better outcomes, many disability professionals try to hold on to their buildings and programs.

Most disability professionals selected this field out of a desire to help people. Some, like me, were students of psychology, interested in a better understanding of human nature. While I have a lot of criticism for many aspects of the system of developmental disability services in the US, this book is not an indictment of the people who work in the disability field. (Although, as in any large system, there are some people who should not be working in it.)

Most of the disability professionals I know work long hours for little pay, and are very much unappreciated for the work they do. In my speeches and trainings, regarding the pay scale, I often tell my audience there are two words they will likely never hear: "nice car." This universally gets a laugh, along with knowing smiles. A colleague once came up to me after a seminar I had given and told me the staff at his agency, which provided vocational rehabilitation, called their cars "rehab cars." "They're all over five years old with high mileage," he said. "We have to drive a lot and can't afford much."

One study reports that in 2003, there were about "874,000 full-time equivalent staff who assist individuals with developmental disabilities in group residential settings, family homes, their own homes, community jobs, vocational and day training settings, and other service settings."[13] The study goes on to project that by 2020, the number of staff needed to meet demand will grow to approximately 1.2 million staff serving 1.4 million individuals. The authors of the report conclude that meeting the future demand will be extremely difficult, citing the current national average vacancy rate of ten percent and an annual turnover rate of approximately fifty percent.

I was paid about $7,200 my first year of full-time employment in the disability field in 1975. By 1978, I had climbed my way up to $8,000. By the mid-eighties, I became a member of an exclusive club – management. I was now an executive director of a multi-service agency, managing more than sixty staff and a multi-million dollar budget. My pay was $29,000 a year, an enormous sum to me – so large, in fact, that I argued with my board of directors that it was too much and the agency couldn't afford it. I recommended it be lowered to $25,000, still a great deal of money. But the board refused to change my salary and I accepted their decision, feeling like I at least had made my point.

It turned out that I was seriously outdone for selflessness. I learned later that year that the agency's assistant director at the time, Janis, who was in charge of our program budget, actually went into the budget without telling me and lowered her own salary, one that I had set for her based on her extraordinary performance. She, too, felt the agency couldn't afford it. And it was hardly a livable wage. Janis was the most caring, hard-working, self-sacrificing person I have ever known in the field. She still is quietly working at that same agency today, and my guess is for not much more than what we paid her twenty-five years ago.

The Other Side of Low Salaries: Exploitation

While pay is always low for those who provide direct services, that is not always the case with the upper management of some disability programs these days. Here is an example of the DIC in action. In 2005, a U.S. Senate Health Committee concluded a four-month investigation into two federal employment programs for people with disabilities.[14] Their findings stated that these programs are not sharing their successes and that executive salaries are out of line with those of the individuals they served. The programs investigated were Javits-Wagner-O'Day and the Randolph-Sheppard programs.

The Randolph-Sheppard program gives individuals who are legally blind contracts to operate food services on government properties. In Javits-Wagner-O'Day, more than 600 provider organizations employ people with disabilities in subcontracts with federal agencies. Many produce brooms, mops, and other items in sheltered workshops. These products are then purchased by the federal government.

The congressional report disclosed that the CEOs of some of the nonprofits make enormous sums, including two examples of salaries at $715,000 and $680,000, citing these as "excessive executive compensation, lavish perks, conflicts of interests, and self-dealing." Also, according to the report, these executives can exploit Javits-Wagner-O'Day contracts for financial gain. "There are no financial incentives to mainstream persons with disabilities." In one instance, the committee found an agency that:

- paid its CEO's consulting company $4.6 million,
- loaned $1.6 million to the CEO's consulting company,
- pledged assets in exchange for discounted CEO Lear jet travel,
- entered into stock swaps with the CEO, and
- paid $2 million to a construction company controlled by the agency director.

An October 20, 2005, follow-up investigative article in *The Oregonian*[15] noted the "cavernous gap" between management wages and the wages of those with disabilities they serve. The article noted that many of the workers with disabilities earn less than minimum wage, and that "those getting rich were supposedly performing a public service. They were 'helping' those who were staying poor – just helping themselves a whole lot more." *The Oregonian's* analysis of the 2004 data from the Javits-Wagner-O'Day program found that less than eighteen percent of the money from the federal contracts went to wages for the workers with disabilities.

I do not believe that the management salaries cited in this case are anywhere near the norm for most agencies that serve people with disabilities, yet the fact that this occurs at all is still unbelievable. While there are examples like this of those who have taken advantage of others, I still believe that the problems in the disability field are largely not people problems. Rather, just as in the institutions, the problems reflect a system that is not coherent and is poorly designed. It is a system that, by and large, has failed most of the people with disabilities who rely on it, just as it is failing most of those who work in it.

How the Disability Industrial Complex Functions

The disability system assumes that people with a certain specific disability need to go to a program that focuses on that disability. "People with autism over here. Cerebral palsy this way. You folks with mental retardation, that door to the right..." The system is organized around the disability. The basic premise is that once you have a specific disability, you need very specific services tailored to your disability. While this can be true, this specificity has been implemented so rigidly that it has produced some unfortunate consequences.

Because a significant disability can greatly impact a person's whole life, people with disabilities generally will need supports to help them live their life. These can include the whole gamut, from cooking, dressing, and taking care of oneself, to getting a job and having a decent place to live. Many of these kinds of general supports for living a quality life have very little to do with a specific disability. One might have unique and highly specific needs regarding mobility or medical support, for instance. But, by and large, the majority of people I have met and worked with needed basic supports. They needed help with living in an apartment, or shopping at a store, or finding a decent job.

But the DIC is not set up according to life needs. It is organized according to the type and severity of a disability. Services and supports flow from disability labels. By using a medical model, the disability system groups people in facilities and programs according to their disability label, their functioning level, or another criteria that is based on some deficit.

There is a huge social cost to this deficit-based approach. To understand this cost involves understanding the nature of discrimination and stereotyping. People are viewed as deviant when they are perceived as significantly different from what is usually experienced. This is part of human nature. When we are faced with someone who is unusual in a way we do not particularly value, we are curious, but also mistrustful.

People with disabilities are viewed as deviant when the community is warned about them, as in this public sign.

This is not limited to disability. I remember the experience of going into a music store to buy some new music. As I browsed among the choices, a young man next to me was doing the same. However, he was very different from me. He was rather large, wore all leather clothes, and had large silver chains as jewelry. His hair was blue and he had many tattoos and earrings in places you can only imagine.

As I looked at him, I felt a bit anxious, even unsafe. His "differentness" was directly linked in my mind to uncertainty and concern about his behavior. When he looked up at me and spoke, I almost jumped.

"Hey man, have you ever heard of this band?" he asked, flashing me a CD.

"Yea, as a matter of fact, I have that CD, and it's really good," I replied, surprised.

"Great. I think I'll try it. Thanks a lot."

As I thought about it, I realized that the same type of initial mistrust I displayed is the root of discrimination. This man did nothing to me to deserve my fear. I simply had misgivings about him based on my stereotypes of people who appeared as he did. This is the root of many social intolerances, including homophobia, racism, and other social problems. And his friendliness made me a bit ashamed of my initial reactions.

The interesting thing about the perception of deviancy is that the "differentness" can be subject to exaggeration. One way to highlight differentness is to group people who share the difference together. What tends to occur is that the shared difference becomes more prominent because it is more noticeable.

If the young man who spoke to me was with six other people dressed like he was, I don't know if I would have even stayed in the store.

Low Expectations

People with disabilities face the same type of reaction. Folks make all kinds of assumptions about their capabilities and their expected behavior because they are different, or deviant, in sociological terms. These assumptions are rooted in stereotypes that have little basis in fact and are damaging in many ways. There is a field of study called "labeling theory" that, although often focused in criminology, is relevant to this topic. In a 1963 landmark book, *Outsiders: Studies in the Sociology of Deviance*, Howard Becker describes deviance as an invention used by those in society who are in power. It is not necessarily due to some act or behavior of the labeled person.[16] When a person violates certain social norms held as desirable by the majority of a society, formal or informal, a deviance label can be given.

That same year, another book was published that established a working understanding for the notion of stigma. Erving Goffman, in *Stigma: Notes on the Management of Spoiled Identity*, described stigma as "an attribute that is deeply discrediting within a particular social interaction." Like Becker, he believed that stigma is based on society's attitude toward a person who does not meet what is desired or expected. That individual is "reduced in our minds from a whole and usual person to a tainted, discounted one."[17]

While neither of these books focused on the disability experience, together they set a foundation to explain how disability is conceptualized in our culture. For people with disabilities, a deviation from social norms can occur because of how they look, act, speak, or learn, or from the way they are treated by the system.

Wolf Wolfensberger, a contemporary researcher who has studied how people with disabilities are stereotyped, has defined several assumptions that people tend to make about those with disabilities. For example, he has stated that people with disabilities are often seen as "eternal children" who will never grow up, as "objects of dread," as "subhuman," or even as a "menace."[18] I have observed people with disabilities experience various versions of these assumptions many times.

Once, I was having lunch with an adult friend named Carla, who has cerebral palsy and some obvious physical disabilities. The waiter came over to take our order. Actually, he took my order, and then he asked me what "she" would like.

I said, "Well, I think you should ask her."

The waiter then bent down, and using a louder voice, slowly said:

"What – do – you – want – to – eat?"

Carla speaks with difficulty, but she is smart and has an amazing array of skills. The assumption by the waiter, who of course knew nothing about Carla except what he saw, was that she was not going to be able to understand him, or possibly not hear him. And so he treated her like a child who is very slow. I am certain he felt he was doing her a kindness, but in fact, she found it hurtful.

If these kinds of assumptions are made in everyday settings like a restaurant, think of the power they have in preventing someone from obtaining a job or an apartment. It's impossible to reach new heights in the high jump when the bar is set too low.

Eligibility and Labeling

Despite its problems, the DIC is a club that can be hard to join. For adult services, there are no guarantees. This often comes as a severe surprise to parents of children in special education graduating from school. In fact, there are wait lists for adult services in most states. In 1998, thirty-seven states reported a total of 46,482 people on waiting lists for residential services or community-based residential placement.[19] In Florida, where I now live, the wait list in 2004 for people with developmental disabilities was approaching 15,000 people.[20] There are similar figures in other states. It is sometimes easy to forget that a waiting list this large is comprised of real people, some of whom are in crisis, and not just numbers.

If the DIC is failing so many people, why are so many others waiting to get in? The answer is simple. People with significant disabilities have profound needs. Families are stressed and want and demand help. The service system offers relief. So they apply. But to be accepted, or to at least get on a wait list, the individual must be found eligible. This generally is accomplished with some combination of testing, observation, and document review, leading to a label being applied that meets some standard of qualification. In other words, you have to be labeled as disabled (and thus open to the stigma of being deviant) just in order to be eligible for services.

From then on, whenever disability professionals read about or discuss a person with a disability, they probably will use the specific term used to describe his or her particular disability. The label might describe a condition: "retarded," "blind," "deaf," "mentally ill," or "autistic." Or it might describe a feature of the person's condition, like "wheelchair-bound" or "trainable" or "hyperactive."

```
There were questions in the mind of the examiner regarding the diag-
nosis.  ████ has had a long standing diagnosis of a learning disorder.
There are other diagnoses that parallel this condition somewhat in-
cluding the persuasive developmental disorder, NOS.  The examiner
elected to go with the diagnosis that has been the case in the past,
hence the following:


Diagnosis:  Axis II  299.00  Autistic Disorder


Prognosis:  For sheltered employment - Fair
```

In this excerpt of a psychological evaluation, a label of autism led the examiner to conclude that the individual's "prognosis" was "fair" for sheltered employment. This kind of thinking has been proven wrong and has been harmful to many people with disabilities.

Knowing the name of one's disability is understandably important to many people. For example, those who struggle with some aspect of daily life may take comfort in knowing there is a name for their condition. It may bring a sense of relief and understanding to the individual or his or her family. Labeling serves several other important functions. It provides a shorthand to others about a person's situation. A label can be highly important for medical purposes, research, or planning rehabilitation. A common body of knowledge can be developed about the condition, because of a shared language.

But labeling a person can be extremely harmful as well. Focusing on someone's challenges and labeling him or her as such can make us forget about the many unique capabilities a person can offer. Over the years, various labels have been used to classify people labeled with mental retardation, including "totally dependent" and "custodial." These terms have taken on very negative meanings and images. Some have evolved into taunts, like "retard." Like most negative labels, they demean people, unfairly stereotype them, and stress differences rather than abilities. Even originally neutral words eventually can become words that convey a poor image for a person. For example, at one school I visited, higher functioning students with disabilities had been classified as "walkers" or "talkers." Although the terms were meant to reflect skills, each had become demeaning and were used tauntingly by non-disabled students. And the implications for those who did not "make the cut" into those classes was demoralizing.

In special education, labeling has produced another concern. About 1.5 million minority children in 1998 were identified as having intellectual disabilities, emotional disturbance, or a specific learning disability. Black and Native American students were significantly more likely than white students to be identified as having a disability. In some states minority students had labels of mental retardation and emotional disturbance at up to four times the rate of white children. According to a Harvard University report:

> *"Once identified, most minority students are significantly more likely to be removed from the general education program and be educated in a more restrictive environment. For instance, African American and Latino students are about twice as likely as white students to be educated in a restrictive, substantially separate educational setting."* [21]

Labels can easily disguise the fact that each person is an individual. Labels also tend to make us predict that people will act in certain ways. People with disabilities do not just face issues related to their disability condition itself. They also face issues of discrimination, misunderstanding, prejudice, lowered expectations, fear, stereotypes, and other social phenomenon related to their disability label. A label applied to a person tends to stick to the person in ways that go beyond treatment. In everyday life, being viewed as a person who is mentally ill, blind, deaf, or intellectually "retarded" carries a whole lot of social baggage.

The way in which a person is introduced to someone relates to how he or she is perceived. Knowing that Artie is autistic might help explain some of his unusual behaviors. But at the same time, the word "autistic" can prejudice people's expectations. This concern is actually reflected in U.S. law. Title I of the Americans with Disabilities Act prohibits employers from asking applicants about their disabilities. Although employers can ask about one's ability to do the job, there is no reason in the eye of the law to know someone's label, because it can (and does) lead to discrimination.

I believe the best way to describe an individual's unusual behavior, appearance, or situation is simple. If the person consents, I talk about what that person needs or uses to do whatever it is he or she needs to do – communicate, get around, breathe, whatever. If a behavior is unusual, I describe what a person might observe in everyday terms, as if it were a personality trait. "When John gets anxious, he..." (repeats things to himself or rocks back and forth, etc.). This is usually understood and accepted much better than saying John is *perseverative* and *self-stimulatory* due to his *autism*.

Throw the Label Away

Over the years, my advice to families and professionals alike has been to leave labels behind. Maybe we are all just too label-happy. It seems to me that there are so many labels for life's problems these days that we all qualify for several – do you sleep poorly, too long, intermittently? Do you eat too much, too little, at odd times? Are you anxious about heights, traffic, bridges, work, other people, wearing clothing, wearing no clothing, sex, having fun, not having fun?

Our field has had such a laser-like focus on deficits, that often deficits are all we can see. A joke I heard once applies here. If a disability clinician were to analyze life, he or she would likely label it a terminal disease (sexually transmitted). I am not demeaning some of these problems, because they can be serious. But sometimes, the label for a problem, once it is applied to you, can take over your life in as many ways as the disability itself, sometimes more.

I remember reading a startling label in the file of a young man. He could speak both Spanish and English, but he used lots of repetitive phrasing, something people with autism sometimes do. (It is called "echolalia," because the person is echoing things over and over again that he or she has heard.) The label was: "pervasive developmental disorder, bilingual-echolalia." Somehow the evaluator had managed to take

a marvelous multi-language skill, which many of us do not
have, and add it to a negative label to make it appear even
more intimidating!

Another example I have is a brochure that purportedly
is trying to promote the idea of employment for people who
happen to have mental illness. But the label used in the brochure copy is a bit intimidating. It reads: "a training and
placement service designed for *chronic psychiatric adult consumers* (italics added) and an exciting concept for...business."

One wonders how many employers in the state are excited
to hire anyone to whom one could apply the word "chronic."
Remarkably, there are those in the DIC who are so comfortable with throwing around their jargon and labels that they
would fail to see how those not of their world might view
such a four-word label as unappealing, negative, and different.

In this country, disability labeling is mandated to get children and adults into a system of support. But once diagnosed
and deemed eligible for services, people should start refocus-
ing on life and what they want for support needs, not their
label and what it implies they need.

Like a medical hospital, the DIC separates (segregates)
people and groups (congregates) them based on their labels.
From the medical point of view, this makes some sense. If
you have an aneurism, you want to go to the specialist and
the appropriate cardiovascular unit at the hospital. But this
makes medical sense because the aneurism is defining your

treatment. However, with a developmental disability, it is probably not a good idea to have the disability define all of your life services. This is a difficult point for many people to understand. They ask, "Aren't you then pretending the person is normal? Aren't you denying that the person has a real problem that needs help?"

The answer to this question is: not at all. A disability will often dictate specific support needs in relation to various things in life, from learning, to working, to living at home, to making new friends. But these areas of life are first defined by each person – where and what they want to learn, where and how they want to work, where and how they want to live, and who their friends are.

Once we know our choices in these areas, we develop preferences. Then we set our goals. Most disability services today approach this backwards. In order to support people, the system places them in segregated places to learn, work, live, and socialize, with perhaps the eventual goal of rejoining society. These are places where people share the same label, the same difference. There is a huge social price paid for this approach.

Labeling Is Hazardous to Your Life

The DIC's response to unjustified segregation has been to say that its services are a continuum that leads back to community life. This is often called the "flow-through" model. The idea is for people with disabilities, as they are taught new skills, to eventually work their way through a series of programs until they are out on their own in their communities.

Let's follow someone who has a cognitive disability as she enters the service system. We will call her Marie, an outgoing thirty-eight-year old woman. Marie has always lived at home and has never been in any formal adult programs for people with disabilities. First, Marie's parents apply for services. Her parents are aging and they think she needs to go live in a home where she will be cared for. They tell the local state office what they want. "A day program would be nice, too," they say.

Marie is referred to someone who will test her and/or review her records to determine that she is indeed qualified as a person with a developmental disability. Once this determination is settled, Marie is given a specific label. She probably will have a report placed in her file stating that she is mentally retarded, with a specific IQ score that will be less than seventy. (Up to seventy-five can be acceptable in some places to allow for standard measurement error.)

Marie's IQ score, along with other factors, determines the level of severity of her retardation. Here is how the American Association of Mental Retardation (AAMR) states it:

> *"Although not perfect, intelligence is represented by Intelligent Quotient (IQ) scores obtained from standardized tests given by a trained professional...mental retardation is generally thought to be present if an individual has an IQ test score of approximately seventy or below...It is important to remember, however, that an IQ score is only one aspect in determining if a person has mental retardation. Significant limitations in adaptive behavior skills and evidence that the disability was present before age eighteen are two additional elements that are critical in determining if a person has mental retardation."* [22]

The Diagnostic and Statistical Manual of Mental Disorders, Fourth Edition (DSM-IV) is the U.S. diagnostic standard for mental healthcare professionals.[23] The DSM-IV classifies mental retardation into four levels of severity, based on IQ:

- mild mental retardation, IQ from 70 to 55/50,
- moderate mental retardation, IQ from 55/50 to 40/35,

- severe mental retardation, IQ from 40/35 to 25/20, and
- profound mental retardation, IQ below 25/20.

One of the first things that jumps out about this scale are the words themselves. For people who are already considered different, words like "severe" and "profound" (much like "chronic" in the previous example) have emotional weight and cannot but add to the stigma they already carry. These are labels that are added to the disability label itself!

It is difficult enough to have a label of mental retardation, and harder still to be labeled by the degree of retardation using some of the scariest words in the English language. These labels now get mentioned in everyday usage. Indeed, the words mild, moderate, severe, and profound were replacement words from the original clinical classifications: "idiot," "moron," "imbecile," or later, when the terms "dullness" or "feeble-minded" were used. Yet these more "modern" labels are often the first thing clinicians, staff, and yes, sometimes even parents, volunteer about people when I ask them to tell me about an individual.

I often wonder how I would do at a job interview, when asked to describe myself: "Well, I am severely Italian, moderately graying, and profoundly impatient!" (Okay, maybe profoundly graying, too!) If I didn't scare off my interviewer by this, I don't know what would. (I once used this example in a seminar. Without a moment's hesitation, a student in front said, "Well, I am moderately Catholic, and still chronically guilty." Some of us knew just what she meant.)

But just as troubling as the words are the implications they carry. It has become conventional wisdom, for instance, that people with severe or profound mental retardation are unable to be employed in the community, or learn how to do most daily life tasks, such as cook or clean for themselves. This has turned out to be largely false, yet the label carries weight. According to the DIC, it dictates the kind of program a person with a disability should be in.

One result of this has been an attempt to direct the classification system away from IQ scores. In 1992 the AAMR proposed a revision to the scale of severity of mental retardation to one based on the level of support the individual requires to function successfully in society.[24] So, rather than IQ, the system used the following four levels:

- intermittent support (episodic need),
- limited support (needed for specific periods of time),
- extensive support (needed regularly for an extended period of time), and
- pervasive support (life-long, intense need).

However, up until now at least, this "levels of support" system has not been widely adopted. The traditional system based on IQ continues to dominate the testing and labeling process.

Grouping People with Similar Disabilities Has a Cost

But getting back to Marie: assuming she eventually moves off a waiting list for services, she will enter the DIC system. In my experience, this means placing her in an open "slot" in a residential and day program where she will be with her "peers." The placement might not be ideal, or even close to ideal. But, unless it is a new program, the placement is primarily determined by where an opening exists.

Now let's consider what it means to be placed in a group of your peers. Webster defines a peer as: "one that is of equal standing; one belonging to the same societal group especially based on age, grade, or status." However, the DIC system generally interprets peer as: "one who shares the same disability label or level of functioning."

The reality of placing people in open slots based on peer groupings is that a number of outcomes emerge. Some are unintended and highly negative. Most peer groupings are arranged for cost-efficiency, especially for programs with higher numbers of participants. Again, as we discussed in the medical model roots of the DIC, putting people who share a label together for treatment seems like a wise use of resources. We can then apply similar treatment to a group of people who share a problem.

Unfortunately, this creates new problems.

First, people's lives, their dreams and goals, while largely impacted by their disability, are not and should not be defined solely by their disability. The grouping model is like saying that all those people who have had their left arms amputated should live and attend day programs only with other right-armed people. Because these are life programs we are talking about, and not just a few hours of therapy a week, this kind of grouping decision has a huge impact on a person's way of life.

Second, grouping people for learning reasons has certainly proven to be advantageous for certain types of learners, especially those who are gifted. They are then surrounded by other creative and intelligent thinkers, which can foster new learning through the modeling of others. But what happens when learners who have difficulty learning are segregated from talented learners, only to be surrounded by learners with challenges? Who are their models? Other slow learners.

This is particularly apparent when we consider certain disabilities. For instance, people with autism are often "treated" for their tendency to avoid certain kinds of socialization and for their unusual and repetitive language. Although autism is a complex disability with many features that vary from one person to another, a common trait is social avoidance. People with autism often do not make direct eye contact and seem to keep to themselves, often focusing on objects of interest, or repeating certain preferred behaviors.

How sensible is it then, in order to "treat" these issues, to surround an individual with these traits with others who also are not likely to socialize and who use repetitive language? The outcome is a home or classroom whose goal is socialization, filled with isolated individuals, most of whom prefer to keep to themselves.

I have also encountered many housing and day programs designed to treat "those with challenging behaviors." These are the individuals who sometimes are violent or disruptive. The reasons for this can be quite complex. In my experience, those who attend such group programs are often quickly contained due to strict guidelines and responses, but are never completely "under control" within the natural environment to which they must return. It is questionable whether we ever come to understand the reasons for their actions by using an approach that often is designed to simply suppress a response. In these programs, there is a constant stream of rule-breaking. The attendees are now provided with other models to learn from. In other words, they learn new inappropriate behaviors they hadn't even considered before from those rule-breakers who surround them. ("Wow, he just threw a chair; I'll have to try that one sometime.")

Getting Lost in the Group

Certainly not all programs are the same, and not all fail at helping individuals learn new, more appropriate ways to behave. But the general premise of grouping everyone with challenging behavior together, I think, makes this task far more difficult than it should be. It adds to the perception that these individuals are trouble. More significantly, grouping with others who share a "problem" can shape a negative self-identity.

I had a friend named Albert in grade school. He was very smart, but had a tendency to goof off sometimes in class. He once flunked an important spelling test. The result was that the teacher referred him to a remedial reading program, largely, I suspect, to have someone else supervise him for a while.

Years later Albert confided in me, telling me that remedial reading consisted of lots of rote memorizing, which he hated. It was taught by the gym teacher, who had little interest in teaching spelling at all and made as many mistakes as the children. Albert said he kept flunking spelling tests, and soon came to believe that being a bad speller was just who he was. And no, he was not dyslexic. He was just in a place poorly designed to correct his spelling problems, all the while surrounded by bad spellers.

He looked at me in exasperation and said: "I couldn't even cheat! Everyone else there couldn't spell either."

Given the stigma of having a disability label and being considered different by others, one would think that disability services should try to minimize further stigma. But instead, the label becomes exaggerated when people with disability labels are grouped together in schools, homes, day programs, transportation, recreation, and nearly every other aspect of life.

People often generate opinions about others based on initial impressions, and then modify those impressions as they encounter new information. When a person has a single noticeable difference, such as a disability, that characteristic can be moderated by other characteristics, such as personality traits, style of dress, and job title.

This idea is reflected by a pioneer of the disability field, Marc Gold. Gold wrote in 1980 that "the more competence an individual (demonstrates), the more deviance will be tolerated by others."[25] This is known as the competency-deviancy hypothesis. Let me explore this further.

Imagine you are meeting, for the first time, a woman in a wheelchair whose speech is a bit slurred. Some people will make assumptions about her intelligence, status, etc. based on the wheelchair and her speech. But now imagine that the individual in the wheelchair is introduced to you as the head of a local company, and that she is wearing a nicely tailored business outfit. The centrality of her disability immediately fades, in light of her status and appearance.

But what can get in the way of this hypothesis is grouping. If you are meeting for the first time a group of eight individuals in wheelchairs, there is no opportunity to process information competing with the disability. Instead, the fact that all of these individuals have a common difference, a wheelchair, is pretty much all that you will perceive. In other words, you don't see a group of individuals, all of whom happen to use wheelchairs. You tend to see a group of wheelchairs, all of which happen to have people in them. You see the stainless steel.

This is exactly what happens to people as they live, shop, and recreate in their communities in groups.

Grouping Exaggerates the Shared Difference

I was shopping at a mall once and, like everyone else around me, I could not help but notice a group of people with intellectual disabilities moving down the aisle. It was a bit of a spectacle. They arrived in a van, moved through the mall as a group, and ate and shopped as a group. They were dressed in ill-fitting clothes, and were basically herded by two staff members who constantly gave out orders to keep things in line. I could only imagine that from above, the group looked like a single organism, an amoeba moving through the corridor. It was difficult to picture how one could perceive individual competence when their collective disabilities were so prominent. Grouping people of like disability only magnifies what they share in common – the disability.

Some will argue that an anti-grouping approach negates people's preferences to be with other people who share their disability. Being careful about grouping individuals with disabilities for treatment and community life does not mean that people with like disabilities should not be seen together or socialize. On the contrary, relationships between people with disabilities should of course be supported when they are based on mutual preference.

I don't see why being sensitive to individual preferences and personal presentation should prohibit friends from seeing each other, spending time together, or choosing to live together, whether they share a disability label or not. But I have to wonder whether people with disabilities have been given opportunities to meet the great range of people who make up the fabric of a community before making choices.

It is the unnatural groupings the system imposes for nearly every life function that I am talking about. When people with disabilities choose to gather together for advocacy, or some recreational event, or to marry, we should of course offer our support.

But grouping people who share a difference (a disability) exaggerates the perception of difference. It limits who will be friends, neighbors, schoolmates, and work colleagues. Lives become defined, not by interests, family, goals, and social relationships, but by disability-related goals often imposed from a program. And in some cases the disability system even labels the group itself!

For example, there is an approach to providing employment in which we place a group of people with disabilities in a business environment to do the work of that company. The workers with disabilities usually are supervised by the disability service agency, and often work in the same physical space. They typically arrive together, take breaks together, and leave together. Sometimes they are even paid by the agency supporting them through an arrangement with the employer, rather than directly by the employer.

This group is known as an "enclave," a group that is distinctly different from a larger surrounding community. One definition I found even referred to an enclave as a haven in *enemy* territory.

Is it any wonder that there are limited interactions and relationships between workers in the enclave and the other workers at the business? It is words like this that imply there is a difference between this group of people and everyone else: a school of fish; a pride of lions; an enclave of the disabled.

At the beginning of this chapter, I noted that I finally left my teaching position; I had left forever my work in large residential facilities that group so many people with a label together. I had accepted a position to run a new program for adults coming out of a state institution called the Laconia State School in New Hampshire, due to the court order for deinstitutionalization.

Dawn was now working full-time and pursuing her master's degree at a graduate school near the job offer, so it seemed perfect. I figured working in a community setting was going to be a huge step forward. In so many ways it was. And yet, as I spent more time getting to know the people the agency was serving, in sometimes just as many ways, I discovered it wasn't.

C H A P T E R   T H R E E

Once Segregated,
Hard to Leave

*"Where many of us worked overtime in past years to
find clever ways of building the avoidance of risk
into the lives of our clients, now we should work
equally hard to help find the proper amount of
normal risk for every person. We have learned:
there can be such a thing as human
dignity in risk. And there can be a
dehumanizing indignity in safety!"*

–Bob Perske

Imagine working in a cubicle all day long, and the end
of the workday comes. As you tiredly emerge from the building where you work, you are greeted with a breeze of warm
and scented spring air that you hardly knew even existed that
day. That was something like the feeling I had on leaving a
job based in an institutional residential facility and finding
myself working in a community program for people with disabilities – a place called the Monadnock Workshop in Peter-
borough, New Hampshire. It was easily the best place I have
ever worked, and many of the co-workers I met there are still
my friends.

One of the best things about starting my new job in community services was getting to meet the people with disabilities I was going to support. Many of them had lived their lives

in the state institution in horrific conditions. As they left and joined our housing programs and the new day program I had started, they seemed delighted.

But there were also challenges. There was Stewart, for instance. He was a rather thin, frail-looking man in his fifties. He could be absolutely charming one moment, then explode in a shower of expletives and threats the next. He had learned to be volatile, I think, because this garnered respect at the institution. The behavior was a way out of doing things he didn't want any part of. He would walk around carrying a stuffed animal and look at you indirectly, warily.

I learned how much Stewart liked sweets, and when I would see him, I would sometimes offer him something. His reaction was pure joy, and he would laugh and light up like I had given him the most precious thing. He and I became friends. He seemed to be aware I was in management, and I often felt he treated me with some sort of respect for my role.

Stuart, in a happy moment.

Joe was another character, in his forties, big and tall. When I would see him, he was like a salesman on a car lot, my new best friend. He would greet me with the warmest smile, saying, "Well, look who it is! Well, hello to you! Yes, yes. Here he is. Joe's new friend!"

I couldn't help but smile back and be glad to see him. But Joe also heard voices in his head. He would unpredictably get upset, and he could be violent and aggressive. He had poor bladder control, and would sometimes resist staff efforts to help clean him up when he had an accident.

Yet Joe and I also became good friends. I could often calm him down when others could not. Dawn and I provided "respite" for the caring people who lived with and took care of Joe. In this case, the respite meant that Joe stayed overnight with us in our home so his caretakers would have a break.

This kind of experience should be mandatory for anyone in management in disability services. It is one thing to work with people who have significant needs in a program; quite another to have them live with you, as I think many families understand all too well. But despite the 2:00 A.M. sheet changes and the constant patter from Joe, it was enjoyable. For someone like Joe, eating ice cream with us after dinner became the highlight of a lifetime, and the experience made us appreciate those small gifts we often take for granted.

Management Inside the System

The agency where I now worked, and where Joe, Stewart, and others came to live and work, was well-respected in the state. We served adults with disabilities, primarily those with intellectual disabilities. This was an opportunity for me to grow, and I was excited about the challenge. This was not a place where doors were locked from the outside, or where large numbers of people lived in one place. There was a recognition of human rights and a respectful tone. It was refreshing. The agency was located in a small town, most of the staff were caring, and it was a time of great change in the field. The agency ran a sheltered workshop, a day treatment program, several group homes, and a fledgling community employment program.

After just about a year, I returned from a vacation to learn that our CEO was leaving. As we sat in his office, he asked me if I would consider applying to take his place. It came as a complete surprise, and I was gratified for his respect of my skills. After a search, and with staff support (for which I will always be grateful!), the board of directors selected me to become its new executive director.

I, of course, had no idea what I was in for. Managing a large human services program produced far more anxiety than I had thought possible. There were budgets to balance, staff to hire and evaluate, complaints to resolve, and services to monitor. Then there were state meetings, policy changes, grants to apply for, and an endless series of meetings with parents, staff, my board of directors, and state funders. There were even natural calamities, such as a flood that pretty much wiped out our ground floor facilities one year.

Fortunately, we had an exceptionally good team of people who worked there. After all these years, I still keep in touch with some of them. But I also inherited a few people (and programs) that did not seem to be working very hard at all – this in a place where there were not enough hours in the day to do what was needed.

Once I walked past the office of one of my program directors and found him with his feet up on his desk, leisurely reading the paper. He had a habit of being late and hard to find. Another time I walked in on another manager casually playing computer games. Neither worked for me for very long. I had to deal with an individual who stole gasoline using our agency credit card, and another staff member who falsified time sheets. I inherited a money-losing and time-demanding restaurant that was supposed to train people with disabilities for restaurant work, only to find very few people with disabilities actually got such a job from their experience.

Although these problems were the exception rather than the rule, it was all very time-consuming and worrisome. Worse, the problems distracted me from my goal of better, more community-focused services. And of course, the fact that we still had people grouped in homes and programs, albeit on a far smaller scale than in an institution, still created issues.

Escape from the Group Home

"Hello?" My home phone rang late one evening; it was a staff person who worked at one of our group homes.

"Dale, this is Dave. Stewart is gone."

"What do you mean, gone?"

"I mean gone. He took off. We can't find him anywhere."

I called the police and quickly headed over to the home. Stewart apparently had run away due to a fight he had with another resident. He had been having some problems getting along with this person. He was also angry at staff for telling him what to do.

Besides the fact that Stewart could get himself into real trouble outside on his own, another significant concern was the weather. It was early winter, and the New Hampshire evenings were getting very cold. We called all the staff we could find and spread out into the area, calling out Stewart's name. As the evening wore on, the state police sent a helicopter with a searchlight, adding to the surreal feeling.

Weary, I returned to the group home and thought hard about Stewart. I realized how smart he could be and how he wasn't likely to put himself in a truly dangerous situation.

While everyone else had extended the search farther from the home, I thought that it might be more likely that he was close by, hiding, and was scared to come back due to all the commotion.

I got the remaining staff to go inside, and I went back outside and hid myself in some bushes. After about thirty minutes of hiding in the cold and dark, and just when I was beginning to question my sanity and wonder what in the heck I was doing for my career, I saw Stewart sneaking around the yard, looking to see if everyone had left. He moved like a cat! I watched him with a mixture of admiration and anger. Perhaps he was returning on his own, or perhaps he was just checking up on the action; there was just no way to tell.

I felt really foolish in some way, like I was a hunter stalking my prey. But if I let him get away and didn't find him again that night, he could die. I lunged for him; he saw me and started to run. I chased after him and ended up tackling him and finally escorting him back to his room. He was mad at me for a while, and I with him. But we soon made up, and life went on. Community life is not without its risks.

Stewart was fine, and he went on to live out his life in his room, his day program, and his visits to town. He was always with his cherished stuffed animals, and still had his occasional flashes of temper. When he passed away a couple of years later, I was one of his pallbearers. The funeral took place on a cloudy winter's day at a stone church located across the street from our agency offices. There was a sense of timelessness to the New England scene. I remember the wind gently swaying the trees against the grey of the sky, and our feet crunching the snow as we carried Stewart to his final resting place.

The speeches at his well-attended funeral were a testament to how he had become a part of our community, self-contained as it was. As I sat at the funeral, looking at all the people in attendance, I realized how different it would have been had he never left the institution. I doubt there would have been anyone there at all to bear witness, at his death, to his remarkable life.

Signing a Weekly Paycheck for Seventy-Two Cents

While the agency often bounced from crisis to crisis, as managers and staff we tried to make good decisions for the people we were helping. Still, despite all the skill and committed staff we did have, I was uncomfortable with several things. Most of the people we served were still living lives very separate from their community. The wages we paid in our workshop were quite low. I was horrified signing my first payroll for the workers with disabilities we employed in our workshop: I found myself signing several checks for less than a dollar – this for a week's work!

I imagined someone going to the bank and presenting a check to the teller for seventy-two cents. I understood at some deep level that what we, the disability experts, were saying was that this is what this person was worth for an entire week of labor.

We were teaching the public that people with disabilities were pitifully unproductive, which is not true at all. Productivity is related to a lot of variables, including motivation and the skills required for the job. We just hadn't done a good job matching those qualities up for some of the individuals we were supporting.

If you are wondering how these low wages could be even legal, in the U.S. a law called The Fair Labor Standards Act includes a provision for a special wage for workers with disabilities. Its purpose is supposedly "to prevent the curtailment of employment opportunities." The Wage and Hour Division of the Department of Labor authorizes special certificates that permit wages for certain qualified individuals that are lower than the minimum wage. In the disability field, this is usually termed "sub-minimum wages."

Now there's an oxymoron for you. We were paying people something less than minimum, a word that means "the lowest you can go!" Wages must be "commensurate with" (equivalent to) those paid to "experienced workers without disabilities employed in the vicinity for essentially the same type, quality, and quantity of work."[26] But the kicker is that the wage must be tied to the workers' productivity.

Suppose a job entails putting together a package, something the average non-disabled worker in that area does making nine dollars an hour. And suppose that the average worker can produce ten packages in an hour. Then this becomes our standard for any worker in the workshop doing the same kind of task. Except our worker, for whatever reasons related to his or her disability, can produce only one package in an hour. That means the hourly rate will be one-tenth of the norm, or ninety cents an hour.

Workshop advocates defend this as fair, and in fact I have seen the use of sub-minimum wages as a marketing tool when appealing to employers for work. The appeal goes something like this: you can get your work done and pay only for what it is worth. But the reality is that the offer comes across like this: *we have a special deal – workers with disabilities will work at 30% off!*

The bigger issue is that the reason many people with disabilities earn so little when compared to a normed sample is that the work is poorly matched to their interests and capabilities. Workers with disabilities aren't always slower by 50%, 80%, or 90% on all work tasks – it depends on the task, the person, and the job fit.

> **Level of Productivity:** On the VIEWS (Vocational Information and Evaluation Work Samples) ▬▬▬ achieved an average percentage of 41% of what a trained worker in industry would produce. This percentage arrived at in relation to predetermined time standards for each work sample (MODAPTS). This places him in the High Work Activities Classification. While performing hand packaging tasks his/her hourly rate was $2.69, which is 52% of the current Minimum Wage.
>
> **Dexterity/Coordination**
> His overall dexterity and coordination were adequate to successfully complete all work samples and work assignments. Specifically he was able to grasp, place, and position objects, and was able to use both hands simultaneously, with right hand dominance. VIEWS work samples used for observation were: Machine Feeding 61%, Mail Sort 41%, Mail Count 37%, Nut Weighing 33%, Collating and Stapling 43%, Stamping 30%.(MODAPTS).

In this excerpt from a vocational evaluation, the individual's vocational potential is judged on a variety of simulated benchwork tasks such as sorting, counting, weighing, and stapling. The conclusion drawn is that the worker's productivity is only fifty-two percent of minimum wage, which is classified as "work activities," a practice vocational training program where the individual is not provided real work for real pay.

Once again, there is also a perception issue with the use of sub-minimum wages. It implies less worth for a whole class of people that society has defined according to their deficits. Recently at a conference, I heard a disability advocate from Wisconsin speak up about how she came across one man in her state who earned an average of one-third of a penny per hour for a total of 220 hours for the entire year. This comes to less than an hour per work day, and a paycheck of less than two cents per week.

America should be outraged that something like this can happen.

A paycheck of two cents sends a message. It teaches people about what and whom we as a society value and what and whom we do not. I understand the position that employers will not hire and pay competitive wages to those who are not as productive. But that assumes that people with disabilities cannot be as productive as anyone else. It turns out, as we will discuss later, that they can be, given creative job matching and support.

More recently, some in the disability community have questioned the usefulness and fairness of the special sub-minimum wage program. Some advocates have called for its end because of the potential for abuse. I agree. Minimum wage should be the minimum – by definition, the lowest you can go. If there is a productivity gap, let us work with the employer to solve it in some way so that the cost does not come out of the pocket of the person who can least afford it – the worker with a disability.

What would I call a well-paid worker in a sheltered workshop? A visitor.

The Flow-Through Model Is Constipated

Besides the wage issue, I was also troubled that very few people in our agency ever moved out of the workshop to a job, or out of the group home to their own place. I soon learned that this is part of the nature of the DIC – one of the most critical and damaging facts about the system is that people generally get "program-stuck." Let me explain. The service system, as I learned, is actually a vast array of agencies, each usually focused on particular kinds of disabilities. And within each agency, there is a program hierarchy, a series of programs based on functioning level, creating the "flow-through" continuum of service mentioned in the last chapter.

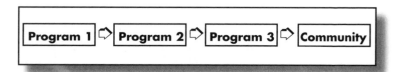

The idea is that people are assigned to a program based on the needs that arise from their disabilities. The program then trains the individual to a higher state of competence, making him or her ready for the next program. Eventually people move into a less supported community setting, such as a job or apartment.

Let's explore how this might work in an employment-focused day program for Marie, the individual we talked about earlier. Marie, if you recall, has finally left the waiting list and has been found eligible for services. She has now been labeled as having severe mental retardation.

Marie is referred to a local agency, likely some private, non-profit organization. It is probably not housed just in a single building where everyone comes. Most agencies host a series of day and residential programs designed to "meet the needs" of people with intellectual disabilities. Typically, people are grouped according to their level of functioning: mild, moderate, or severe/profound.

The people with the most severe disabilities usually attend a "day treatment" or "day habilitation" program, where they learn "daily living skills" including hygiene, dressing, and the like.

People with higher IQ scores might be introduced to the idea of vocational training. They might be given "work activities," which provides practice work. I have seen people in these programs sorting objects such as colored paper or hardware. Or they might place several small items in a bag and seal it. The point is to have them do repetitive things to get used to the idea of work.

Those who are more capable are able to work in the sheltered workshop. Here people can work on real business contracts subcontracted to the agency. Pay is based on performance, and sub-minimum wage is generally allowed. Once the sheltered workers build their skills and work tolerance, the theory goes, they will be "job-ready."

Placing pegs into a pegboard to "practice work skills." Photo from *Christmas in Purgatory* courtesy Center on Human Policy, Syracuse University

Since Marie has no work skills or experience, it is decided that she should start out by attending a day treatment program, where she will be exposed to work activity. Staff explain to her parents that as she progresses, she will move through to the next level program, eventually maybe even getting a real job.

This sounds good – a sensible, slow-paced build-up of skills for Marie, as she slowly moves from more restrictive programs into the community. But as we have discussed, this approach has several problems. Most notably, it begins with a grouping of people who share the same label. In addition, all these individuals are now segregated from everyone else.

And what about the premise of people moving through the system from one program to the next? Well, here the model breaks down completely. Research has shown that less than five percent of the jobs people with severe disabilities obtain in the community have anything to do with the typical workshop tasks of assembly, packaging, or manufacturing.[27, 28]

There is admittedly little hard data on movement rates, except for a few state studies from the early 1980s.[29, 30] These indicate movement rates of one percent to three percent per year. There may be some exceptions to these very low movement rates in various parts of the country. But as someone who has spent thirty years visiting many states, and as one who directed agencies, a sheltered workshop, and a day habilitation center, my own experience is that people seldom, if ever, graduate from the day habilitation, day activity, or work activity programs in which they started.

Conceivably, at this rate, if you entered the flow-through system at age twenty-two, when most schools no longer fund special education programs, you might be in your seventies before the disability service system found you a job. "Congratulations; now we will get working on your retirement."

I remember sitting in on a meeting between a family and an agency. The family was quite upset that after fifteen years their son still had not had a job opportunity. The staff of the agency patiently and condescendingly explained how the flow-through model worked. The mother, exasperated, said, "But there is no movement. Your system is constipated!"

Instant Readiness

Unfortunately, and at the risk of taking this metaphor too far, the answer to a constipated system is not to administer a laxative so that people will begin to move. The whole system is flawed from top to bottom. This is because it flows from a premise that we need to focus on people's deficits in simulated, segregated environments, albeit in community locations.

One of the reasons it is so difficult to move into the next level program and eventually into the community is that the DIC functions on the basis of "readiness." People with disabilities have to meet a set of criteria before they are considered ready to move on. These are often termed "pre-" skills, as in pre-vocational, pre-community living. Let's return once again to Marie.

All of her adult life, Marie has wanted to live in her own apartment. She loves music and dreams of being a singer. She volunteers these dreams to the teacher in her new day activity program. Often life dreams of people with disabilities are simply dismissed as being a fantasy. But in this case, a kindly staff person tries to "reason" with Marie.

"Well, Marie, we have an independent living curriculum, and we will see where you should begin," he says. So they complete a rather lengthy checklist of all the skills Marie needs to be able to live on her own in an apartment. The list is comprehensive, ranging from cooking and shopping, to housekeeping, money management, personal hygiene, and safety.

"Marie, there are lots of things here you simply don't know how to do. We will begin at the beginning. As you learn more things, then maybe you will be closer to ready to someday, maybe, have your own apartment."

"OK," says Marie. "That would be great."

But the reality of this readiness list is that it is insurmountable for Marie. She gets stymied on the first skill set, money management. She is easily confused by coins and change. It might take years of practice for her to learn to count correct change. The DIC believes that this is just the reality – that people like Marie need lots of time because progress will be slow due to their disability. We must be infinitely patient as she builds her skills.

And after money management, then what? She will need to master basic cooking, cleaning, fire safety, and on and on. It is apparent that Marie will never see the inside of her own apartment. She is deemed not ready until she can demonstrate she has mastered a list of skills – skills some professional has decided people like her need to be independent.

Once at a conference in San Antonio, Texas, I spent a memorable dinner with author and disability consultant Herb Lovett. He explained to me his metaphor for how this system of small steps by measurable objectives doesn't work for people with disabilities. He said, "Imagine you have five people who are drowning at the bottom of a six-foot-deep pool. The first goal the disability system will come up with is to get them all two feet off the bottom – no matter how long it takes."

You Don't Have to Master Shoelaces to Wear Shoes

Obviously, this kind of thinking, a building up of skills with very small steps leading to independence, is seriously flawed. Few among us are truly independent in all aspects of life. People with disabilities, like all of us, need some support in order to manage their lives. For many with more challenging disabilities, this support can be significant. It can also enter into areas that non-disabled people can do for themselves, such as bathing or cooking.

But *people with severe disabilities do not necessarily need to be able to achieve competence in all the skills associated with each area of life, as long as there is the necessary assistance set up*. Sometimes this support must be creative. For example, while Marie might have limited money skills, she could still shop and manage a budget with help. Perhaps she might need an account with the local grocery store. Or perhaps she could have a credit card with a small limit. Or maybe she could shop with someone – a friend, a neighbor, or a paid staff member whose job is to help her.

Each of the obstacles in Marie's way to her own apartment can be dealt with in the context of achieving what it is Marie

wants. Her goal is the premise, and her support the means to
get there. This is compared to the DIC, which prefers to see
the goal as the achievement of a whole host of skills, step-by-
step, from a long-term plan that might never get there.

A simpler way to look at this is to examine the choices we
make for each thing we must negotiate in life. We can either
spend years teaching someone how to tie his shoes, or we
can help him to select loafers and Velcro sneakers. If the DIC
was evaluating me, I would not have been a talented enough
cook to qualify for my own apartment in college. Thankfully,
I was free of that type of influence, and I managed to come up
with alternative eating strategies. (And by the way, I am now
a pretty good cook.)

Sometimes we learn what we need; sometimes we come
up with a work-around. It is okay to spend some time getting
ready for things that require a high degree of skill, but it is
not okay to spend too much time trying to be ready for the
simple things in life: a job, a home, and good friends. These
should be givens, and we should be able to get to these areas
of life as soon as possible.

You Should Taste Spinach to Know If You Hate It

And there is another factor that limits movement. Most
people, especially those who have had limited experiences (such as people with severe disabilities), tend to want to
stick with what they know. When I first went into the Laconia State School and met with some folks with disabilities to
talk about their moving back to their community, there were
several who refused. I was probably naïve in not expecting
this, but it surprised me. Some of these folks had few or no
personal possessions and lived on a ward with twenty other
people. At first I could not understand their response, given
their living conditions. But for people who have lived their

whole life in an institution, it is really all the life they know. For many people, moving to something unknown is scary.

Many advocates for continued institutionalization use this as an argument for maintaining institutions. They say that people's choices must be respected, and that some people choose to live in an institution.

But with choice-making comes a responsibility to understand the options you have. Consider the following conversation, common to most parents:

"Eat your spinach."

"No. I hate it."

"Have you ever tried it?"

"No. I was born hating it."

People have to taste their choices to really understand what they don't want and might want. We need to help people be informed about their real options. People need to make informed choices based on good information. They need to have the time and experience to understand what their options are. For the people who initially refused to leave their ward, we set up visits to the community. They spent time in homes and places where people lived and worked. They eventually got comfortable with the idea of moving, and were even excited by the prospect of having their own rooms, TVs, pets, new friends, and maybe jobs.

Ultimately, everyone did leave the Laconia State School. Interestingly, I don't remember ever hearing any of the thirty or so people I got to know in this process saying they wanted to return to the institution once they were out.

What about those who still might choose the institution after experiencing community life? Assuming the experience was handled well, I think this is a difficult dilemma. It is likely only a very small number of people we are talking about. But I also think our public obligations for providing choices has limits. *And the institutional choice is an expensive, tax-payer-funded, obsolete model of service that has unethically segregated a whole class of people.* I think this is especially telling when there is an alternative that has better outcomes.

But in the early eighties, as the director of one of those alternatives, a community program staffed with caring people, I realized that we were still not fulfilling what people truly needed. Sure, our programs were smaller in scale, more personalized, and situated in real community settings. But while it seemed as if we had done some great things for people by setting them up in this way, we had come only halfway. We still spent too much time on readiness and trying to move people through programs. We still had people in separate buildings, places where people *without* disabilities did not typically go unless they were paid to be there. I realized that the DIC encourages agencies to confuse the worth of their facilities with the value of people.

John O'Brien, a thoughtful commentator on disability service systems, stated my feelings well. He wrote:

> *"The recent experience of a large number of people with mental retardation is better described as movement from one kind of institution to another than as community integration. Many community alternatives perpetuate undesirable practices, such as deprivation of purposeful activity, isolation from ordinary places and people, crowding, lack of choices, and failure to provide individualization."* [31]

I believe there are seldom any good reasons for separating people in order to help them with their lives. We certainly have reached a place in our society where we at least recognize the moral inadequacy of separate facilities based on race, religion, or ethnicity. Separate is not equal, nor can it be made equal.

Yet people with disabilities represent the last bastion of lawful segregation in housing and employment. Do we know of any other minority group that has a high unemployment rate where our answer has been: "Here is a separate building where all of you can come and earn an average of less than minimum wage doing whatever work we can find when we can find it?" I doubt any other minority group would stand for that.

Lou Brown, a respected advocate for community services for people with disabilities, perhaps said it best. Focusing on making people master "pre-skills" (for example, pre-vocational training) has proven to be a waste of time. In his words, "We cannot wait for people with disabilities to learn what we have decided are the 'pre-skills' because it turns out that 'pre' means never!"[32]

If we wait for someone with a significant disability to master everything needed to live, work, and play in a community, there is almost no chance he or she will ever get there. This person will *spend a lifetime getting ready for life.*

And the tragedy is that is exactly what is happening for untold numbers of people with developmental disabilities right now.

CHAPTER FOUR

Abusive Responses to Challenging Behavior

*"I began to see how behaviorism could be used as a
political tool that really supported a hierarchy of power
between therapists and those they ostensibly served."*
—Herb Lovett

Jason looked around the room and said, "Jason is on the launch pad!"

Back in 1978, when I was still working as a teacher of children with autism at a residential facility in New Hampshire, I taught a student named Jason. A tall adolescent, he, like some others with autism I have known, referred to himself by using his name rather than using the pronoun "I."

Suddenly, he looked at me in the eye, crouched down, and yelled, "Jason is going to explode!"

Over the years, I worked with many people with disabilities who acted in ways that were difficult. Some were aggressive, others refused to follow directions, and still others behaved in ways that were not socially acceptable to the time or place. Jason's tirade continued.

"BBRROOOM! There he goes. Jason is OFF!!!"

Jason was someone who presented such challenges. He would often refuse to do his work. If he was unhappy, he would launch into a fit of excitement that eventually could lead to hitting himself so hard that he hurt himself, a phenomenon known as self-injurious behavior.

From the very beginning of my career, I was taught to approach people like Jason as "problem people." Because behavior like Jason's is learned and influenced by the environment, we were taught to analyze the setting and how people like him interacted with it. In Jason's case, I learned how to deconstruct his behavior into its component parts. This way, once we discovered what was signaling him to act or what was responding to him to keep acting this way, we could make adjustments.

This primarily consisted of analyzing what happened in the setting before Jason acted, while he acted, and after he acted. You can greatly influence and even control behavior if you manage events before, during, and after. There is a whole technology called behavior management that is based on these principles. Controlling events in the person's environment undoubtedly influences the way a person behaves. And when you break complex situations down into small bits, you can build new learned behavior, one step at a time.

As a quick review, anything that occurs after a behavior that makes that behavior more likely to happen again is known as a reinforcer. From social praise to money, reinforcers increase the rate of behaviors that precede them. You also can increase behaviors by removing a disagreeable stimulus. ("I will turn off the music you dislike when you finish the dishes.") That is called negative reinforcement. There are lots of complex relationships between reinforcers and behavior, depending on the quantity and timing of reinforcement. Small changes in these variables sometimes can have large effects on the individual.

A punishment is the opposite of a reinforcer. Something that happens after a behavior that makes the behavior less likely to occur is called a punishment. The event, in effect, appears to suppress the behavior. Using punishment to control behavior, however, can produce all kinds of difficulties and ethical concerns.

Summary of the Relationship of Behavior to Consequences

Consequence	Adding	Terminating
Positive event	Reinforcer- Behavior increases	Extinction- Behavior slowly decreases
Negative event	Punishment- Behavior decreases	Negative Reinforcement- Behavior increases

The Problems of Reductionism

The principles of behavior technology, when used judiciously as a teaching tool, have been a huge boost for the education of people who have cognitive disabilities. People with cognitive disabilities can learn fairly complex tasks using simple, step-by-step procedures that build on one another. But this technology also can be used to control social behavior that we do not approve of. By manipulating events, we can suppress or discourage behaviors we do not want and encourage the likelihood of behaviors that we prefer.

While this approach often works, it also has proven to be fairly intrusive, as well as unfairly simplistic. Because the basic relationships between behavior and what happens before and after are usually discernible, professionals are confident they are managing a situation when they manipulate these events. But behavior is far more involved than managing events before and after. In fact, events and their relationship to behavior can get quite complex. Think of all the things that can influence how we act: hunger, fatigue, general health, feelings of pain, emotions, heat, light, attention, distraction, and so on. This is not to mention our history with a given situation or the people in it, or the feelings we have in reaction to our situation. The illustration below shows just a few of the other factors that can influence human behavior besides the consequence that immediately follows it.

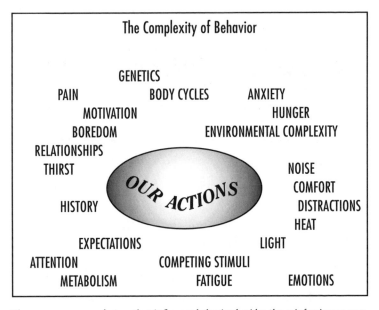

There are numerous factors that influence behavior besides the reinforcing or non-reinforcing events that follow behavior. Sometimes these factors can modify or even negate the effect of controlling consequences contingent on behavior.

Too often, behavior plans push all this complexity aside in the rush to develop a treatment plan. There is a tendency to do something that is easily controllable, by managing one or a few elements of the environment. But what if something else is going on? For Jason, I came to learn there were at least two things going on related to his alarming behavior. One was inside his head, where he focused compulsively on rockets, explosions, and the like. He was fascinated by this theme, and wanted to endlessly explore it. Another thing going on was that he was terribly bored by school and the academics that were being pushed on him. His behavior was to retreat into his head and fantasize about rockets blasting off. And, when made to refocus back to work, he would begin to actually act out explosions. If he worked himself up enough, he even would begin to hurt himself. None of these things were within my control.

What had been tried on Jason was a parade of behavior management plans: Do this, and you get this. Don't do this, or you will lose this. If you get loud, you will go to "time out." None of them worked, because none meant as much to him as the events in his head. And his emotional response to people making him do something also was too strong. But the rule of thumb was, as soon as Jason starting making any sounds like a rocket, send him to "time out."

Behavior Change Should Include Trust First

Slowly, I got to know Jason. As he got comfortable with me, we began to have some fun together. Soon I decided to reject the rule about not allowing him to explore his fantasy. I allowed him to do it within limits. I told Jason that when he got too excited, it disturbed other people. So as long as he could control himself, he could make his sounds and fantasize about rockets when we were not working.

What's more, at social times, I even started to engage him when he started talking about this, asking him when he was taking off and how high he would go. This went against everything in the book about not reinforcing behavior we wanted to go away, and some of the other staff were visibly shocked. ("You are encouraging his inappropriate behavior!") But unless I had control over all sources of his reinforcement, it mattered little what I did, unless I were to punish him severely. Jason loved our conversation, and it cemented our relationship. I could see his body relax as we talked. He would start just the beginnings of a smile, all the while looking at me out of the corner of his eye. We shared his inside world in just a small way, but I was being allowed in. Instead of his fantasies spinning out of control, I was able to participate in them and then redirect him back to reality. Because he loved my engagement, he saw me differently from others in charge. I became someone he could trust.

My relationship with Jason is at the heart of what I believe behavior change is all about. I think we have to understand behavior in terms of its communication, and that we should have a trusting and authentic relationship to influence behavior. Because Jason came to trust me, he came to trust my advice about when it was okay to fantasize, and when it was not. And when he worked himself up, I was one of the few people who could enter his world and help him climb out of it. Over time, his fantasies became less and less frequent. We had regular conversations about rockets, the Space Shuttle, and when things explode. But it no longer was an aberrant behavior that could lead to self-injury. It was just a passion of his.

While I am not advocating that therapists join in with all people who engage in delusions or fantasy, I do think we should acknowledge their existence as the first step in building our credibility.

The Abuse of Time-Out

Over the years, I have been a part of situations where there was not enough time spent on establishing a trusting relationship with a person whose behavior was painful to others or to him or herself. Instead, there was a reliance on simplistic control programs, such as "time-out," as was used originally on Jason. Time-out is philosophically and technically a concept based on neutrality. It is supposed to be neither reinforcing nor punishing, and it can be quite useful. You can interrupt a dangerous chain of behavior by asking the person engaging in it to step away from what he or she is doing. The idea is to take away all stimuli and consequence to a behavior. This usually involves sending the individual to a secluded area away from ongoing life activity, such as a "time-out room" or a "seclusion room."

The theory of time-out goes back to learning theory. It is based on the fact that removing any possible reinforcement during an inappropriate behavior will lead to the "extinction" of that behavior. That is, the behavior will slowly fade away. In fact, extinction is a very predictable response when you take away something that has been reinforcing a behavior – first, the behavior usually abruptly accelerates, then slowly decreases. After a while, it reoccurs briefly again, as if it has a "test" spurt. This is called spontaneous recovery. After that, the behavior rarely occurs at all. Behaviorists have documented the phenomenon in numerous settings, such as with pigeons pecking at a light and reinforced with food pellets. When the food is stopped, there is a flurry of pecking, then a slow decrease to nearly nothing, followed by a last gasp effort, and then no more.

But because behavior is so complex, and because humans are not pigeons, setting up a time-out program does not work this way. In fact, this model is rarely how a time-out program is actually set up. I have seen many time-out rooms in my time. They are barren by design. There usually is a way to see in to observe the person in the room, but not a way to see out. Again, the concept is to remove all stimuli so there is nothing reinforcing.

In actuality, many time-out programs can be highly aversive. Here is an excerpt from an actual behavior plan I have regarding time-out:

"If Sue will not go to time-out, she will be assisted to the time-out area by two instructors, each holding one of her forearms and putting another hand under her arm and walking her over to the time-out area."

Of course, few people wish to be placed in seclusion, and escorting someone there can easily become a wrestling match. On the other hand, I once watched as a teacher dragged a young lady into time-out for some infraction, and the young lady was laughing while the struggle ensued. She obviously enjoyed the physical attention. How non-reinforcing is that?

Time-out is another one of those DIC programs that has a solid theoretical basis, but is not well-connected to what happens in the real world. In practice, it plays out as a punishment used to implement control by someone in power. It is not just an unequal relationship; it is a way to exercise power in a highly unequal relationship.

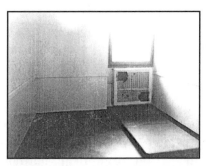

This grainy image of a seclusion room was part of the photographic evidence in the court ruling for the closure of the Pennhurst State School and Hospital in Pennsylvania in 1978.

Punishment to Control Behavior: An Invitation to Abuse

Still, you might ask what is wrong with time-out as a punishment, if it is effective in suppressing challenging behavior. First of all, punishment is very difficult to use successfully for long-term learning. Research has shown that punishment needs to be applied immediately after the behavior and be relatively intense to have the desired response.

These two simple criteria are often a source of trouble. Delays in punishment limit its effect on the problem behavior, especially with those unable to cognitively understand the relationship between the punishment and the undesirable behavior. And providing an immediate response is often difficult. If you end up punishing too long after the fact, the results will be negligible.

Also, if the punishment is not strong enough to immediately suppress the behavior, you run the risk that the individual learns to take in the punishment without changing, so that the next time he or she will need a much stronger response. People thus can learn to tolerate high levels of punishment, because they have been applied a step at a time.

Imagine punishing your child for stealing something. The punishment is to send him to his room for an hour. If the punishment isn't strong enough to stop him from stealing, he will do it again. (Perhaps, in behavioral terms, because he doesn't get caught all the time, the reinforcement of the stolen item is strong enough to offset the risk of receiving the punishment. Of course, there might be many other reasons for stealing that this does not account for, but whatever the case, he steals again.) So the next time he is caught, you make him stay in his room for half a day. This still turns out to be insufficient. Now, because he is building up a tolerance for the punishment, it becomes harder and harder to use a punishment of sufficient impact.

For punishment to work, it also must be consistent, and there must be no way to escape. Consistency often is nearly impossible in a human service world of changing staff and rotating shifts. And escape and avoidance are known responses to punishment. If the learner manages either one, what he or she really has learned is the escape response to the punishment, rather than not to do the problem behavior.

I have vivid memories of my then twelve-year-old cousin Marty, who kept getting in trouble with his father for eating a whole box of cookies at once. The first floor of their house had cellar steps in its middle, and you could circle around the walls that contained it. His father, discovering the crime and threatening punishment, would chase him around inside the house.

He caught him the first couple of times, but soon the punishment became a threat from which Marty had learned to escape. He eventually figured out how to circle those cellar steps, stay out of reach of his father, and make his way to the basement and out of the house through a basement door. The chase itself, which happened frequently, became hilarious to watch, with Marty running at full speed, both fear and laughter in his face. The whole process never stopped him from looking for and eating all the cookies.

But these kinds of issues are hardly the real concern to me. The problem with punishment in general is that it precludes the formation of a trusting relationship because of the inequality present. It teaches what not to do and whom to watch out for, rather than what to do and whom to trust.

And there is something else. When I worked at my first job in the autism residential facility, punishment was a big part of the learning program we were taught to use to control certain behaviors. Simply yelling "No!" when someone did something wrong changed me emotionally. If my punishment didn't work at first, it became a power struggle. I would feel the need to win. My heart would thump and my threshold for inflicting more punishment would be easier. In other words, the punisher becomes worked up and can lose sight of self-control. And when the episode was over, I had won, but I felt awful, emotionally drained, and not very happy with myself. The punisher gets punished, too.

Another example of this at the autism facility where I worked was how they instructed us to handle children who had toileting accidents. According to the director, cleaning a child up in a warm bath or shower after such an incident would only reinforce the inappropriate toileting accident. Instead, we were to give the child a "cold shower." I witnessed several of these showers, and they were incredibly punishing, as staff would yell at the child while splashing very cold water on their body to clean them. It was a highly emotionally charged event, and very humiliating for the child.

When punishment is used in any relationship with a person with a disability, I usually see the use of threats develop quickly. People who are managing their behavior primarily because of implied threats are not in a good situation. Consider what happens when the specter of punishment is finally removed. The suppressed behavior often returns.

This is why speeding tickets are so ineffective to control all those cars flying past you on the highway, or to control *you*, if you are a speeder. The system is built around punishment. Install a radar detector, and the threat is diminished enough to be ineffective. What happens when someone is caught speeding? The driver may slow down for a little while, but then before long he will be back to his old ways, perhaps watching a bit more carefully for a police car. Punishment, unless it is severe, generally has a temporary effect.

I have witnessed professionals debating setting up a behavior program in response to a student with disabilities presenting challenging behavior. The choice was fashioned around whether a person "needs" a punishment program or a "nonaversive" program, identified as time-out. To me, this is like asking whether we want all-out nuclear war or a limited nuclear exchange.

Bad Application of Reinforcement Is Just Bribery

Because a lot of programs have acknowledged the problems of using punishment, I have witnessed a lot of staff people setting up situations to reinforce people with disabilities to stop problem behavior. ("Alberto, if you stop yelling, you can earn...")

Rewarding "not doing something," whether it is problem behavior or not, is not behavior management; it is much more like bribery. How easy is it to ever get rid of a program that rewards non-behavior? As soon as the bribe is gone, the stage is set for the behavior to return, unless incompatible behavior that is desirable has been rewarded. This point is a little difficult to grasp. Suppose a teacher has a child in class who has repeated tantrums. After several days of this, the teacher pulls the child aside and offers him an ice cream at the end of the day if he has not had a tantrum. Sound familiar? I see parents try this kind of thing all the time, but it is an invitation to disaster.

The "deal" might work at first. But as with any bribe, there is an unequal relationship. This time the teacher (or parent) is not really in control. Because there is no reward for behavior, but rather a reward for non-behavior, the teacher will have difficulty eventually getting out of the promise. (Where did my ice cream go? I guess I will have to act up to earn back the deal!) It also teaches the student, not to mention all the other children in class that have been good up until then, that to get the ice cream, you first have to act in an unacceptable way.

So this leaves us with reinforcers. But here again, trouble can ensue, because professionals feel they must be able to completely control all the possibilities of reinforcement. I once called a group home to talk to Craig, a resident there with whom I was working. He had a number of behavioral challenges. The staff member who answered said, "I'm sorry, Craig cannot talk to you today."

"Why not?" I asked.

"He didn't earn you."

The group home staff had set up a review of all Craig's reinforcers in order to manipulate them to get Craig to change his behavior. I came up as one of those reinforcers. For Craig, not being "good" meant not earning the right to talk to me.

This was way out of line. My response was, "Put Craig on the phone. Right now."

Again, this attempt at managing reinforcement reveals an unequal relationship, not to mention an unjust situation. While certain things in life are indeed reinforcers, not everything should be subject to manipulation in an effort to change behavior. I would put basic food, sleep, and privacy on that list. I also would include access to friends and family. Craig shouldn't need to earn me, no matter what he had done. If anything, it was probably more important than ever for me to be able to talk to him if he was having difficulty. Unless you are adjudicated by our criminal justice system, certain things in life should just come without any strings attached.

Behavioral Jargon Can Disguise Reality

In the early eighties, I came across a journal article that discussed *"paradoxical interventions"* used with individuals with intellectual disabilities who presented undesirable

behaviors. The term was used to describe a behavioral tech-
nique in which the "client," meaning the individual with a
disability, would be, counter intuitively, *encouraged* to perform his or her maladaptive behavior under more controlled
circumstances. Among the interventions described, one in
particular stood out.

The article described a male resident of a group home
who prided himself on his appearance. According to the article, he had taken to screaming in order to gain staff attention. (One wonders what his home environment was like for
him to develop such a coping mechanism.)

The intervention consisted of the staff telling him that he
was now to scream as much as possible. But that's not all. He
was told he must also wear a clown suit, since he was obviously the house clown. The staff went on to buy him an outfit
and insist that he wear it. At house meetings, they repeatedly
referred to him as the house clown. After a short while, he
reportedly stopped screaming. Another behavioral success.

It is easy to see how dressing up this professional abuse in
clinical language such as paradoxical intervention hides the
reality. Failing to learn the cause of the resident's pain, what
he was screaming about, or putting forward ideas about why
he felt compelled to act that way is horrendous. To believe
that this resident somehow reframed his actions because of
some mysterious psychological effect of treatment is unjustified – he was being humiliated and punished severely. Consider the imposition of such control over a human being in
his own home such that he would be forced to wear a clown
suit.

Although this particular example occurred over twenty
years ago, I still find it astonishing that it was considered fit
to be published at the time. I believe this type of nonsense
still can occur as long as professionals continue to mask their

"interventions" with clinical language that sounds somehow respectful. There might well be a therapeutic case to be made for paradoxical interventions of which I am unaware, but if any approach is carried out in the manner described in this example, it should be rejected before it gets started.

Beyond Reinforcement to Explain Behavior: Looking at the Source

Behavior problems seem to crop up more often in disability facility-based programs than anywhere else. I will always remember visiting a pre-vocational training program for people with severe disabilities many years ago while I worked in New Hampshire. I was there was to observe someone who wanted a job. My role was to get to know him and his capabilities and interests. Before I went into the facility, I was warned about being distracted by several people who were considered "behavior people" and who were "acting out."

When I entered, I saw about twenty people sitting at various tables. In front of the people were different practice work tasks. These tasks included sorting different colored plastic items, putting nuts and bolts into bags, and counting out small pencils. No one was doing anything, though. They were all watching the drama going on in one corner of the room. I immediately looked over and saw several people who had been grouped together at a table. ("Ah, must be the 'behavior people,'" I thought.) The staff member in charge was struggling to handle their screaming and throwing of supplies and one person who kept trying to leave.

A staff person came over to me and said, "Please just ignore what's going on there. Each person has his own program. If we give them too much attention, they will just keep acting up."

And indeed, the staff person in charge was all over the table, first moving one person back to his seat, then warning another, then telling the next he had "lost a point." It seemed to me to be fruitless, and, at the least, exhausting for everyone.

Later, when the day was over, I came over to learn about what the people were actually supposed to be doing.

"It's pre-vocational training. Everyone here has to meet a production standard on the work that is assigned for the day," responded a staff member.

"Well," I said, "what work were they doing?"

"Today, this table was assigned a clerical mail task."

"Do they get paid?" I asked.

"No, it is practice work," she answered.

"And what did they have to do?"

"Well, the first person has to fold this stack of paper like a letter. He piles up his finished work here. The next person puts each letter into an envelope here. Then the next person seals the envelope. Then the final person unseals the envelope and takes it out again. We have to reuse the materials until they get damaged."

My jaw hung open, but she didn't seem to notice.

"Of course, because I am certified as a behavior specialist, we have all the behavior problems at this table," she continued.

"I noticed."

"Yeah, Bob likes to leave his assigned area. Ronald screams a lot. Steven rips up our materials sometimes, and Carl can be aggressive. He has been hitting Steven lately."

Unfortunately, this kind of situation exists in too many programs. We have missed the forest for the trees. The analysis of behavior has deconstructed each problem action, and like a laser, tried to fix it. But consider the situation for Bob, Ronald, Steven, and Carl. They were all labeled as having

mental retardation, and each had difficulty with verbal communication. Behavior was their way of expression, and no one
was bothering to listen.

The work they were asked to do was completely void of
meaning. Not only that, it was never-ending, despite their
efforts. Before their eyes, whatever they had accomplished
was simply pulled apart so they could be forced to complete
it again. And why? To receive some sort of social praise from
a staff person with whom they had no real trusting relationship.

I am not saying their behavior was an appropriate way to
respond to frustration in a work setting, but it was absolutely
understandable. If I were in that line-up, I could easily imagine having much the same response if I had difficulty communicating and no one was listening anyway. The first thing
I would try to do was to escape (Bob). If that didn't work, I
might scream to voice my displeasure (Ronald). If that still
didn't work, maybe I would just get rid of these materials.
(Steven). As a last resort, I would probably feel the same urge
to punch out the guy who keeps giving me the work I just
finished! (Carl).

As I looked around the room, I realized that it was not a
time-out program, or a point system, or any other program
that was needed here. These people were bored and unhappy. Their style of communication, while not socially acceptable, was clear. Rather than enforce compliance, our response
should have been to stop and learn from the way these individuals were acting. I would venture to guess that if Bob,
Ronald, Steven, or Carl were in a real job that they cared
about, and had developed some relationships with the people
they worked with, many of their behaviors would magically
be "cured."

How People Act Is Communication

People's behavior can communicate all kind of messages. Sometimes people with disabilities who otherwise have difficulty communicating tell us things we wish we didn't have to hear.[33]

I am tired, bored, lonely, upset.
I am hungry, thirsty, sleepy.
My tooth hurts, my stomach aches.
I don't like you.
I don't like this guy next to me.
I want to stop now.

Or their behavior may be trying to communicate something else we will never know. But the important thing is to try to understand. I have nothing against structuring learning environments to encourage people to have teachable moments in which they can begin to understand how their behavior can affect others and themselves. But there are many other things to consider changing first. It is just that changing a person's life – where he or she lives, works, or plays – can be a lot more involved than setting up a system of reinforcement or some other program. So, few people want to take that on.

With the increased use of supported employment and supported living, people with more significant disabilities are in more integrated community settings. When they behave in socially unacceptable ways, our job is to help them understand the implications of their behavior and to learn to change how they act. But the tools we use also must be naturally valid – there must be minimal stigma and social acceptance to the technology we apply in community settings.

If Theresa works at a restaurant, and if she loses her temper too easily, she will have a much greater risk of not making any friends, and of potentially losing her job. But I have witnessed the response to change this scenario often miss the mark. For instance, I have seen workers like Theresa wear "smile stickers" for good behavior. When they obtain five, they can then go buy a soda for their break. Earning symbolic rewards that can be traded for a reinforcer later is participating in what is called a "token economy." If they lose their temper, they lose a sticker. The sticker is the reinforcer used, and it is traded for the highly valued primary reinforcer of the soda. The loss of the sticker is technically called "response cost," and it has similarities to punishment, though milder.

The theory is sound, and the effect on the behavior is predictable. But the social perception of Theresa has been damaged considerably. None of her other co-workers wear smile stickers. No one else had to earn a soda through good behavior, or lose it through bad behavior, for that matter.

This program has no social validity in the place where Theresa works, and it adds to her stigma as a worker with a disability. Her temper is indeed a problem in developing positive relationships. Ultimately, so is her behavior program to control it. Alternative solutions might involve counseling, behavioral rehearsal of the difficult situations, or a more natural reinforcer of sharing a soda at break with a friend who reminds her how well she is doing to control herself when things are frustrating.

A Little Knowledge Has Proven to Be Dangerous

It might be difficult to learn what a behavior means. We might not always have the answer, but we first need to learn to respect what people are trying to say. We should listen and think before we respond. Critics might point out that a comprehensive analysis of behavior will include a much more sophisticated consideration than the examples I have provided.

Of course they should. The problem is, while that may be true in theory, in my experience it seldom is the case in practice and often still omits key aspects of life.

The principles of behavior change are well-rooted in good science. But their application can be as bad or worse than what they are trying to improve. We need to ensure much better oversight in the use of behavior technology on the lives of vulnerable people.

There are several new movements in the field of behavioral support that recognize the shortcomings of the approaches I have described. The use of "positive behavioral support" and the study of the "communicative aspects of behavior" are key elements of this trend.

I think that behavior change works best when the behavior is first understood and put in context. All too often, little effort is put into this first step. If the goal is to help people make significant changes in their lives, then we should figure out how to do that. We should help people in need of behavior change develop relationships with others they can trust and respect. And then, if there is agreement that a specific strategy is needed, we should come up with a respectful approach that everyone agrees on. But we need to make sure it not only will work, but will meet socially and culturally acceptable norms and ethical considerations. This technology is far too controlling and powerful to simply yield to.

C H A P T E R   F I V E

Dangerous People:
Public Attitudes and Myths of Disabilities

*"I am not suggesting that everyone should be like us.
Our gifts are rare, and that is good. But, as difficult
as our bodies and minds can be, their very unique-
ness brings strength and positive challenge both to we
who live in these bodies and minds, and to society –
when we are appreciated, respected, and celebrated."*

– Judith Snow

In the late 1980s, I read about a trend known as "dwarf-tossing" that had emerged in college bars across the country, and especially in Florida. It appeared to have originated in Europe. Dwarf-tossing was a contest in which competitors would actually "toss" a person with dwarfism. The person with dwarfism put on a harness and was then spun around and thrown onto mattresses placed on the ground. The thrower who could toss the person the furthest would win.

The participants said it was harmless and that those they tossed were willing. And perhaps it was all meant in fun. But

I wondered how anyone could not see the cruelty of treating a person as an object just because of his or her size.

There is actually a long history of public perceptions of people with disabilities as undesirable, less than human, dangerous, or child-like. This is despite a Harris poll finding that almost half of the public knew individuals with disabilities as friends, relatives, neighbors or co-workers, and "almost a third have a close friend or relative who is disabled." But, reported Harris, "It is equally important to stress the even larger numbers who lack this familiarity." According to the poll, most Americans still feel awkward, embarrassed, or apathetic around people with disabilities. "The emotions that are most universal are pity and admiration...of how they have overcome some of the consequences of their disabilities."[34]

Depending on the disability, there are great differences in how comfortable the public is when confronted with a person with disabilities. Mental illness causes the greatest unease, followed by facial disfigurement, senility, and mental retardation. Hearing and visual impairments and the use of a wheelchair produces considerably less discomfort.

Integration Is Not Just the Absence of Physical Segregation

So the paradox is that while we now know that people with disabilities should not be segregated away from their communities in institutions or other facilities, many of their communities have negative stereotypes and discriminatory attitudes. In the mid-eighties, during my years in New Hampshire working to develop community services, I came across all kinds of discrimination.

For example, discrimination can happen at an early age for youngsters with disabilities. People with developmental disabilities often are seen as not having any potential. The cost of their education is viewed as a burden that takes away from non-disabled students. In a meeting of concerned taxpayers held in Keene, New Hampshire, residents complained about the cost of educating children with disabilities, and termed special education a "monster." The headline in the local paper the next day ran: "Special Education Turns Into Monster." The image of a monster associated with students with disabilities is a damaging combination. The implication is that not only is the program monstrous, but so are the people in it.

Around the same time, in Hillsborough, New Hampshire, a feature story on special education ran in the local paper with the headline: "Education Tariff for Handicapped Angers Taxpayers." The word tariff was an interesting choice. It conveyed the idea that there was a necessary extra fee or charge citizens were forced to pay. The concern was that special education programs deprive non-handicapped students of their "fair share of educational resources."

Education tariff for handicapped angers taxpayers

Actually, the situation is a bit more complicated than pitting special education costs against the costs of educating students without disabilities. The federal government in 2002 provided eighteen percent of special education funding (although by law, the federal commitment is supposed to be forty percent).[35] While states vary, most provide another significant share to local governments, leaving local communities to fund what is left. This varies widely by state, but the point

is that the costs to local government to fund special education are usually not so excessive as to preclude the quality of
the education of other students.

But it was this sentence in the "tariff" story that really got
to the heart of the matter:

> *"Should our money be used to educate the child who may*
> *become a teacher or a doctor or to educate a handicapped*
> *child who may become able only to brush it's (sic) teeth?"*

There is a lot packed into that message: these kinds of
kids can't learn. Why bother? It is a waste of time and money.

But perhaps most telling was the use of the language "its
teeth." Not "his" teeth or "her" teeth, but "its." As though this
wasn't really a person we were talking about – someone like
you or me. It was something else, not worthy of our efforts to
provide a public education.

The law in effect at the time of the article, Public Law 94-
142, the Education of All Handicapped Children Act, stated
that all children were to be provided a free and appropriate
public education. It was tested to the limit in New Hampshire, in a court case known as *Timothy W. vs. Rochester,
New Hampshire*. In this landmark case, the parents of a child
with multiple disabilities advocated for the right of their son
to continue his education regardless of the severity of his disabilities.

The court described Timothy as being born in 1975, two
months premature. He weighed four pounds at birth and immediately had respiratory difficulties. After months of hospi-
talization for intracranial bleeding, hydrocephalus (fluid on
the brain), and seizures, he was discharged from the hospital.
By this time, he was diagnosed as having severe developmental retardation, with suspected hearing and vision deficits.

Tim's physical and apparent mental development was dishearteningly slow. His school district continued to defer his eligibility for a school program. In 1984, Tim's mother sued and the court sent the case back to the New Hampshire Department of Education. The state ruled that Tim qualified for special education. The hearings officer held that the "special education laws entitle all handicapped children, regardless of the severity of the handicap, to special education." The officer further ruled that inquiry as to whether a child might benefit from special education is no longer relevant.

The case wound its way to the U.S. Court of Appeals, where the findings were clear:

> "The language of the Act could not be more unequivocal. The statute is permeated with the words 'all handicapped children' whenever it refers to the target population. It never speaks of any exceptions for severely handicapped children...The language of the Act in its entirety makes clear that a 'zero-reject' policy is at the core of the Act, and that no child, regardless of the severity of his or her handicap, is to ever again be subjected to the deplorable state of affairs which existed at the time of the Act's passage, in which millions of handicapped children received inadequate education or none at all. In summary, the Act mandates an appropriate public education for all handicapped children, regardless of the level of achievement that such children might attain." [36]

Regular Education vs. "Irregular" Education?

This decision reaffirmed the right to a free and public education. But the reality is that in most school districts this still translates to segregated special education, often in completely separate buildings. Some school systems are trying to be more inclusive, having children with disabilities join what they term as "regular" education classrooms with the support they need to learn and grow. It turns out there are a lot of benefits to everyone with this approach. The child with a disability is surrounded by good learning models and potentially wonderful opportunities for socialization. The non-disabled children learn something important about valuing diversity. There are many approaches and opinions about the best way to accomplish more inclusive classrooms, with varying terms and associated advantages and disadvantages. But the general idea is for kids to learn to appreciate each other's gifts and differences, and this is a good thing.

This is our best hope for the future, I think, at least in terms of breaking down stereotypes about people with disabilities. When I was in school, we never saw students with disabilities. They were in separate buildings or classrooms. When they came out to the hall or cafeteria, it was as a group. And as a group they looked so different from everyone else. It was difficult for them to just blend in. They were subject to teasing, sometimes cruelly. In retrospect, I think the teasing and name-calling was more about the fear of the unknown that all kids have.

I think that the cruel teasing is one of parents' biggest concerns in having their child with a disability attend school with non-disabled children. But if integrated education starts early, supports build and friendships are made. Kids will speak up for their friends. It definitely can work.

The Language of Deviance

One of the reasons I think people with disabilities have an aura of being unwanted is the way they are described in language, media, and humor. Messages are given in numerous ways. I still have a newspaper clipping in which someone wrote to "Dear Abby," the advice columnist in many U.S. newspapers.

> *"Please tell me what to do when a friend has had an ab-normal child (a Mongoloid). I certainly can't send a card or gift of 'congratulations' to someone who has had such a tragedy. Would a message of 'sympathy' be more in order? Or should something like this be acknowledged at all?"*

Here is someone wondering whether it is right to even acknowledge the birth of a baby with Down Syndrome. And what does a message of sympathy imply? The use of the word Mongoloid to describe a person with Down Syndrome is an archaic term; people with Down Syndrome can have facial characteristics that some believed resemble people from the Orient, hence the term Mongol. The term can be traced to an 1866 book by John Langdon Down, *Observations on the Ethnic Classification of Idiots*, in which he wrote:

> *"...the very large number of congenital idiots are typical mongols. So marked is this that when placed side by side it is difficult to believe that the specimens compared are not children of the same parents."* [37]

A number of like characterizations came out in the media when the Americans with Disabilities Act (ADA) was being considered by the U.S. Congress in the late eighties, through its eventual passage in July, 1990. Earlier that year, James Kilpatrick noted in an editorial that the bill is "limping along" through Congress. It was probably unintentional, but seeing "Bill for the Handicapped Limps Along" in the headline was disconcerting. Even though the verb references the bill, it sits right next to the word "handicapped" and manages to imply an inability to keep up.

Associations such as these might appear insignificant, but psychologists have found they can influence thinking subconsciously. For example, in one study individuals were subliminally exposed to stereotypes with words flashing on a computer screen for fractions of a second. Participants were assigned to either a positive or negative aging stereotype group. Those in the positive stereotype group were exposed to words such as "wisdom" and "creative." Those exposed to the negative stereotype group saw words like "senile" and "dying." The study found that "negative stereotypes of aging may contribute to health problems in the elderly without their awareness."[38]

This isn't just political correctness. Language can certainly shape attitudes, even when it is subtle.

Depicting Disability as a Burden and Danger

Another stereotype relates to the excessive costs of supporting people with disabilities. We have discussed already how this is often cited in public education, but it was also used to fight the passage of the ADA's anti-work discrimination features. For example, in 1991, I spied an editorial cartoon that ridiculed the cost of compliance with the ADA by showing a NASA spokesman pointing out ten billion dollars in needed modifications for the space station in order for it to meet ADA compliance.

Interestingly, there are good data that detail what it costs to accommodate workers with disabilities. Almost half of the accommodations needed by employees and job applicants

with disabilities cost absolutely nothing. For those accommodations that do have a cost, the typical employer expenditure
is around $600, according to a study conducted by the Job
Accommodation Network (JAN), a service of the U.S. Department of Labor's Office of Disability Employment Policy.

But really, depictions of burden pale in comparison to the
fear that can be generated regarding violence in the workplace by people with disabilities. In 1997, I came across a cartoon from the *Richmond Times-Dispatch* by Gary Brookins
that really captured the fear of dangerousness in potential
workers with disabilities. It is a hiring situation in which
a supervisor sits at a desk, facing a government bureau-
crat from the Equal Employment Opportunity Commission
(EEOC). The EEOC official says:

*"No, you may not ask a job applicant about a history of
mental disabilities – that's discrimination."*

The applicant stands behind waiting, holding a large axe
menacingly and wearing a hockey mask reminiscent of the
frightening movie character Jason in *Friday the 13th* horror
movie.

Is there any truth to the notion that people with disabilities are more violent in the workplace? There is no firm evidence that I am aware of to support the notion that people
with intellectual disabilities or any other developmental disability are more violent than non-disabled people. Indeed, at
least in the area of the workplace, there have been so few of
these individuals able to access jobs that there is little data
to go on. But with the increased numbers of people with disabilities going to work in recent years, I have not been able
to find any evidence of these individuals posing any kind of

physical threat. On the contrary, there seem to be far more cases where they have been harassed.

The issue seems to center around mental illness, the disability with which the U.S. public is most uncomfortable, according to the Harris Poll of Public Perceptions. A compilation of research by John Monahan in 1992 at the University of Virginia School of Law found that people who were actively experiencing psychotic symptoms, especially those who abuse drugs or alcohol, had a modest increased risk of committing violent acts. Overall, however, the study found that factors other than mental illness were much more significant predictors of violence. For instance, the combination of male gender, young age, and lower socioeconomic status is a far more powerful predictor of the risk of violence.[39]

However, the reality is that it is terribly difficult to predict which individuals might become violent based on demographics. Though some workplaces do try, the prediction cannot be made with any confidence. Most companies do have policies prohibiting threatening behavior. And the ADA allows employers to set a standard that workers may not pose a direct threat to the health or safety of others in the workplace. "Direct threat" is defined as a significant risk of substantial harm. But the important thing is that such a standard must apply to all employees, whether or not they have a disability.

Again, it is also the case that someone who has a psychiatric disability can be the victim of abuse. For example, in the mid-nineties, Eric Stewart was an employee at Bally Total Fitness. He was diagnosed with bipolar illness and was out of work for a week. When he returned, his colleagues called him "psycho," "wild man," "schitzo," and "freak." He filed a lawsuit against Bally in 1999.[40]

There is a long history of media depictions of people with mental illness as scary, dangerous, and violent, from tabloid headlines ("Freed Mental Patient Kills Mom" screamed a headline in the *New York Post* in 1980) to movies titled *Psycho* or *House of Crazies*. A government report summed it up as follows:

> "*Stigma refers to a cluster of negative attitudes and beliefs that motivate the general public to fear, reject, avoid, and discriminate against people with mental illnesses. Stigma is widespread in the United States and other Western nations. Stigma leads others to avoid living, socializing, or working with, renting to, or employing people with mental disorders.*" [41]

The Service System Supports Disability Myths

While it is easy to condemn the media for producing stories, movies, and graphics that perpetuate negative stereotypes, the sad truth is that the disability service system also does its share. Many agency names, logos, and marketing messages are designed to elicit pity. This portrays people with disabilities by highlighting their deficits and differences. This is exactly the opposite of what an agency role should be, to my mind.

A lot of times this image-making is tied to fundraising. How do you get people to send money to your struggling non-profit? One way is to make them feel sorry for the people you support. I once received a fundraising letter from an agency in New Hampshire that was attached to a purported "profile" (see next page) of the typical person they were supporting. Circled in red for emphasis were the words: "*Irreversible condition – requires constant custodial care.*"

This is the same agency that tries to help these people find housing and jobs in their community. The fundraising message seems to oppose the message that people with disabilities belong and can contribute.

1. NAME: ████████ Carol _____ 2. NO.: ████████
                FAMILY NAME   GIVEN NAME

3. D.O.BIRTH: __3/██46__ 4. D.O.ADMIT: __4/2/46__ 5. SEX: __F__

6. PRIMARY DIAGNOSIS: __Profound mental retardation (Mongoloid)__

7. PLACE OF BIRTH: __Nashua__   __Hillsborough__   __N.H.__
                     CITY   COUNTY   STATE

8. FATHER: __Ronald ████████__   MOTHER: __Died during childbirth__

   DATE OF BIRTH: __3/1/26__   DATE OF BIRTH: __4/16/27__

   OCCUPATION: __Laborer__   OCCUPATION: _____

9. NAMES OF ALL SIBLINGS, THEIR AGES AND WHEREABOUTS:

   NAME   ADDRESS   SEX   AGE
   None

10. FINANCIAL STATUS: __$1500.00 donated by father towards her care.__
11. LEGAL STATUS: __Assigned Public Guardian__
12. AUTHORIZATIONS: __Public Guardian ████████__
13. SUMMARY/CONCLUSIONS: __Irreversible condition. Requires constant__
    __custodial care. Prognosis for improvement extremely poor.__

Not Welcome in My Neighborhood

Another very common mode of discrimination is that of neighborhoods not welcoming people with disabilities into their midst. This is actually a rather complex issue. On the one hand, a lot of terrible misrepresentations have been made about what would or could happen if a few people with disabilities came to live in a neighborhood. But on the other hand, nearly all of the highly contested situations have focused on group homes, housing from four to eight or more individuals, plus staff. A group home can differ from a typical home in a number of important ways, including staff, licensing, exit signs, and the fact that a rather large number of unrelated people who all share the same disability will be living there.

The truth is, few people will welcome a human service program to a residential area, regardless of who will be living there. I think that fact alone is understandable. The character of a neighborhood is important to the people who live there. It is hard to say whether the complaints are based on the misinformation people have about people with disabilities, or their probably on-target assessment that this home will be very different from all the other homes in the area, and that is of concern.

And in one case, it was the state government itself that provided a seriously negative impression of a group home to the public. In 1991, the state of Connecticut established a very impressive sounding Legislative Program Review and Investigations Committee. The function of this group was spelled out in an announcement for a public hearing on conducting studies of the locations of "undesirable" and "controversial" facilities. Examples of these were named in the memo and included: prisons, power facilities, telecommunication towers, hazardous waste facilities, radioactive waste disposal areas, landfills...and "group homes for the mentally retarded." The implied message is that the value of the people with disabilities living in Connecticut's group homes was equivalent to hazardous waste and garbage.[42] In another twist, in 1991, the mayor of Toledo, Ohio, suggested moving people who are deaf near the Toledo airport to cut down on noise complaints.

But let us move past this to focus just on the things people have expressed concerns about related to people with disabilities themselves. While I was working in New Hampshire, there were numerous instances of neighborhoods protesting the arrival of people with disabilities. In one memorable situation, a group of about forty Franklin, New Hampshire, residents (a town I lived in for a couple of years) organized a protest meeting in response to the news that four individuals with retardation were going to move into a home there. According to a press account, the residents said that "while they do not oppose the concept of returning the mentally handicapped to the community, they think their neighborhood is a poor choice."

This is what is known as NIMBY (Not In My Back Yard) Syndrome. Many people will agree with a concept (people with disabilities can live in a neighborhood), but do not want this concept to play out in their very own neighborhood.

A major complaint by the Franklin citizens was that no one told the neighbors of the proposed home in advance of its residents moving in. This is an interesting demand. I don't imagine I would send out announcements if I were moving to a neighborhood that didn't welcome people of Italian descent, like myself. What would it say? "I am planning to move to your area. If you have concerns, you might want to organize now."

The next complaint was "the indiscriminate placing of these group homes in a highly populated area, near a park and school." The assumption, again, is that people with disabilities should not live in populated areas, and God forbid, especially not near a park.

The state had planned to lease a four-bedroom ranch house, but soon dropped the plans. One of the most striking accusations was that the residents with disabilities would be highly dangerous, with residents stating they feared for the safety of their children. In a petition presented to the city, the neighbors said:

> *"We don't think these special people should be placed so prominently where passing children are apt to make unkind remarks which may cause anxieties to build up to a breaking point, at which point their he-man strength can be almost impossible to subdue."* [43]

Was the accusation based on a history of violence from these individuals? Not at all. It was based on a stereotype that people with intellectual disabilities are dangerous – a stereotype that has no basis in fact, nor was it based on the individuals, whom the neighbors had not met. So who were these individuals who dared to try to live in this neighborhood? Three of the four were over 65 years old, and the fourth person used a wheelchair to get around. Not one could conceivably represent a physical threat to anyone.

The neighbors seemed to get especially angry when told that the residents of the home "might come outside on warm days to sit in the sun." I still do not understand how this was perceived as threatening. Perhaps the grouping effect we have discussed so overwhelmed this neighborhood that it could not get past the notion of disability. But even so, their notion of disability was terribly wrong and terribly unfair.

And the irony of it all? The proposed location of the home was 52 *Freedom* Drive.

Establishing an Independent Voice

I had now spent a couple of years as the executive director of an agency, and I was drained. Dawn would find me mowing the lawn three or four times a week just to burn off the stress I felt from my job when I got home. Besides being the love of my life, my wife is a terrific person who has always supported me in my work. Thank goodness she was able to see what my job was doing to me. She helped me gain some much needed perspective.

I felt the programs at my agency were heading in a good direction, and I decided to accept an offer to provide training and consulting in other parts of New England. At first I joined a consulting agency. But I soon decided that I needed to be completely independent. My views about more "normalized" services and my anti-segregation stance were getting so strong that I felt I could be most effective as an independent voice.

So I spent the next couple of years traveling, speaking, and training, mostly throughout New England. I focused on helping the staff of other programs to consider helping people leave day programs and workshops for jobs, or leave group homes for smaller, more personal apartments and homes.

My message was always based on this concept: if society views a person with disabilities as deviant, it should be important for disability programs to minimize the perception of deviancy.

How do people perceive someone who has a difference? Generally, they initially judge how he or she appears and acts. For many people with disabilities, certain aspects of their appearance are beyond their control. People with Down Syndrome, unless they undergo controversial cosmetic surgery, look different. People who use wheelchairs, have an unusual walk, or speak with difficulty all appear different in some way.

Does this mean it is impossible for people with disabilities to escape the label of deviancy? Not at all. Most people do not focus on just one aspect of a person. Unless overwhelmed by a feature so dominant or unusual, they consider the totality. They ask questions: where do you live? What do you do for work? What do you do for fun? They appraise your personality, your dress, and who your friends and family are. If someone has something different about him or her that is not particularly valued, there also may be some other things that are.

And therein lies at least part of the answer.

CHAPTER SIX

Competency, Commonality, and Social Glue

"Our 'map' had assumed that personal and community well-being was produced by institutional systems. This assumption inevitably led to a research focus on management, technology, and funding. And of greatest importance, it led to a de facto classification of local residents as 'clients' – the recipients of institutional services... while omitting communities and citizens."

–John McKnight

Leaving behind my role as a manager at a single agency meant leaving behind daily direct contact with people with disabilities. Fortunately, in my consulting work, I was still able to connect with people through the agencies who hired me. This broadened my perspective a great deal. I now visited numerous agencies and met far more people with disabilities than ever before.

These experiences served only to reinforce how often the DIC was failing people. In the late eighties I did contract work for: individual programs; "area agencies" (regional entities responsible for funding and overseeing services in an entire area through various other agencies that were sub-contracted to provide services); a university (The Institute on Disability at the University of New Hampshire); state agencies, includ-

ing state offices for developmental services; Developmental
Disabilities Councils; and other organizations.

At one point, I agreed to sign on as a temporary executive
director for an area agency in New Hampshire while it conducted a search to fill the position. Once again, I experienced
first hand how a bureaucracy such as the DIC can be dysfunctional and distracted from its mission. Within days I was dealing with major personnel issues, from a manager whose job
performance I felt was beginning to be impaired by an alcohol problem, to a staff member who unexpectedly broke into
tears while I interviewed her for a promotion she wanted. (I
can have high expectations of staff, but I have never brought
anyone to tears before or since.) Once, during a meeting with
some state finance people, an assistant manager nodded off in
the middle of the meeting. This behavior was not disability-
related; it was apparently pure boredom for her. The snoring
was the last straw.

Again, most of the staff were dedicated, hard-working
people trying their best. But the few who presented issues often drained away the creative energy needed for change. I was
happy to have my temporary tenure there end. I returned to
consulting life again. This kept me on the road a lot, and I
probably learned as much as I taught. And after a while, after
seeing sheltered workshop after workshop, and group home
after group home, I came to the conclusion that the system
was far too entrenched to really change in any significant
way.

Escaping the Group Mindset

Our culture values people who are productive, skilled, attractive, and affluent. For a number of reasons that have little
to do with the people themselves, these attributes rarely are
connected to people who are disabled. Rather, they often are

wrongly perceived as people who are incompetent, "funny-looking" children who never grow up, or as even dangerous or sickly.

But the reality is that children with disabilities grow into adults with the same needs as everyone else – interdependence, privacy, accomplishment, sexuality, and responsibility. Individuals with disabilities can learn a diverse range of valued skills. They have demonstrated their on-the-job productivity and their ability to manage a home, given the right supports. Although a disability can make one's appearance "different" from the norm, a more important reason some people with disabilities look different is because they have never been taught grooming or fashion, the programs in which they find themselves are demeaning, or the people helping them do not think appearance is important.

Yet as we have discussed, the myths are powerful. Some neighborhoods have fought against people with disabilities living in their midst. Some people say they are uncomfortable having their children attend school with students with disabilities, or shopping alongside consumers with disabilities, or being near co-workers with disabilities.

The history of professional disability services often has supported these myths. By segregating people, by grouping people together, by labeling people, by creating "special institutions" or "special schools," we have made individuals appear even more different.

I have gotten to know many individuals with disabilities over the years. And in all that time, most of the people with whom I have worked have not asked me to focus on making their disability "better." Few of them, in fact, were overly concerned about learning lots of new skills. If I had to name a problem most wanted help with, it would be loneliness.

I know that is a simplification, but when I talk to people, what comes across is that they want a meaningful life, to have fun with friends and family, and to do something that makes them happy. These are universal desires, of course, but they are manifested differently for each individual.

One of the mistakes we make in human services is to believe we can pre-define what people need. We have standards that are based on "the average person" for employment, residential life, socialization, mobility, speech, and on and on. So our approach is to continue to test, evaluate, and assess people against our standards of normalcy. "How do you stack up to the average?" we continually ask people with disabilities. And when there are gaps, we need to develop goals, measurable objectives, and methods to remediate.

But often these goals and objectives have no personal context for the individual. They are *our* perceived goals and objectives, not the person's. And there sometimes is an incestuous relationship between the evaluator and the paid service provider. As an agency director, I often asked why an individual was receiving a certain therapy. The answer was usually because the therapist who specialized in that area had evaluated the person and determined a need.

Well, sure. Try going to an insurance agent to see if you have adequate insurance. Or ask a hair dresser if you need a haircut. Generally, a need can be discovered.

Now before the letters of indignation from the various therapeutic specialists start, I really do not believe that most specialists are consciously padding their incomes or trying to generate unnecessary paid work. I have a lot of respect for their in-depth knowledge and their ability to help people with specific obstacles. But I do think we are misusing their expertise when we ask them to evaluate a life based only on their area of focus. (This trend isn't limited to disability services.

Witness how specialization in medicine often leaves the patient with conflicting advice, or medicines that could interact with detrimental effect.)

The missing context is to know what accomplishments will make the person happy and productive, and will lead to meaningful relationships and meeting personal goals. Just as important is where these things will occur. For instance, in a program I visited, a physical therapist had concluded (based on an evaluation) that Juan needed to develop the ability to climb steps. As a result, I found Juan in a day program where he practiced step-climbing on a three-step stair purchased from the agency budget for this purpose. Juan did not enjoy this practice, and he tended to resist, leading to the beginning of a new label of "uncooperative."

But step-climbing skills are only important if Juan has somewhere to go with steps – a bank, a job, a library, a store, or his home. Getting to those kinds of places was actually the more important goal for Juan. Being able to climb steps leading to a door only mattered if the steps existed as an obstacle to a place he needed or wanted to go.

It turned out that there were actually only a couple of places where Juan needed help with going up steps. For a person who needs to negotiate so many obstacles, why spend so much time focused on just one? Instead, why not learn to climb where the actual steps are, where you are motivated to succeed? At the store where he worked, because the steps were few and spaced easily, and because there was a railing, he actually could climb quite well. At a hobby shop he liked to visit, it appeared he was going to need assistance gaining entry no matter how much "practice" he had in his day program. So why waste his time with artificial steps that might never take him out to the real world?

Why Not Wasting Time Matters

I think time is of the essence. Over the course of my career, I never feel worse than when I see people waste time in a constant state of getting ready for life. They never reach real life, mind you; they just spend their lives getting ready.

When I was Dirk's guardian, he was still of school age. The program he attended and lived at was required to develop a transition plan for his "individual educational plan," or IEP. The plan came to me one day in the mail. I was never invited to a planning meeting, or called to be asked for my input. Nor, apparently, was Dirk.

Let me remind you about Dirk's situation. He had few possessions and no real friends. His family was no longer involved in his life. He had little experience in the real world, and he often acted in unacceptable ways that could be aggressive or violent. Given this scenario, I would think there were lots of important areas of his life to develop, areas related to employment, community life, shopping, cooking, and socializing. I would expect there would be an exploration of his aptitudes and interests, a plan to build on those things he was good at, and a learning approach that would help him negotiate his adult world with more success.

Instead, the goals sent to me included naming the planets of the solar system and the continents. This may be good knowledge to have, but at this stage in Dirk's life, it was hardly inspiring stuff to change his life. His anticipated post-secondary outcome was to attend an adult training center for adults with disabilities (i.e., a sheltered workshop) – not a goal or an outcome I personally would accept for any student with a disability in my charge who is leaving school.

I believe that no special education student who leaves school should have to transition to a workshop ever again. But they still do, and in pretty large numbers. I think this comes back to the disability focus on deficits, labels, and expectations.

When Deficits Become the Focus

In one of the seminars I used to give as a trainer, I would sort the attending disability professionals into "treatment teams" of about five people each. Each person would be assigned titles, such as "vocational trainer," "physical therapist," "residential specialist," and the like. I would then present them with a case study. Here is an abbreviated version of a needs profile for M.J., a man of about sixty:

- needs to reduce non-compliance and other socially maladaptive behaviors;
- sexual exhibitionist;
- uncontrollable tongue thrusting, also skips childlike;
- unpredictable, needs to be the center of attention;
- expresses dark urges;
- views women as objects; and
- weak social skill development.

The teams then met to come up with a plan of action. Some teams were quite creative, describing behavioral plans that were very extensive. I heard people describe approaches using time-out rooms, punishment, and a medical regimen. Nearly always, when discussing employment or housing, the conclusion was that M.J. needed a very structured setting, most likely a sheltered workshop and a twenty-four-hour monitored home.

When everyone had presented, I revealed that the person for whom they just developed a treatment plan was already known to them.

M.J. is Mick Jagger.

God knows what they would have done to Keith Richards.

Sure, Mick has demonstrated for many years now that he can act in lots of "inappropriate" ways, according to some cultural norms. We can describe them clinically, even give them labels if we want. And as disability professionals, if we focus on these deficits, we probably will want to develop programs and treatment to correct them. But does anyone believe that Mick Jagger is unemployable? Hardly. It has cost me hundreds of dollars to go and watch the Rolling Stones perform.

What the simulated teams didn't know were the context and Mick's unique gifts. Really, in theory, no one should agree to even go along with my seminar exercise. People should be outraged to be asked to develop a plan for someone they hardly know, and for whom they certainly have inadequate information. Yet, no one has a problem with trying to solve M.J.'s difficulties. It is, after all, what we are trained to do.

Too many of the plans I have seen are just not going to change the life of the individual in question in any meaningful way. There is a joke about the well-known phrase, "shit happens" that I think applies here, with some slight modifications:

In the beginning was THE PLAN
And the plan had OBJECTIVES, but they were without Form
And THE PLAN was without Substance
And darkness was upon the face of the Family

And the Family spoke among themselves, saying:
It is a Crock and it Stinketh
And the Aide went to the Instructor and sayeth:
It is Excrement and it is Strong

And the instructor went to the Program Manager and sayeth:
It is a Vessel of Fertilizer, very Strong
And the Program Manager went to the Assistant Director and sayeth:

It contains that which helps Plants grow Strong

And the Assistant Director went to the Executive Director
  and sayeth:
This PLAN promotes Growth and is Powerful
And the Executive Director looked upon the PLAN and saw
  that it was Good
And this is how Shit Happens.

Intimidating Jargon Masks Reality

This fix-the-deficit approach is difficult to challenge because the plans, labels, and approaches are always couched
in impressive terminology. Every field has its jargon, but the
DIC seems particularly prone to it. I attended a meeting once
in which a group of disability professionals was discussing
a young man's aggressive behavior. A behavior analyst was
speaking at length, and to the best of my recollection, this is
a piece of something he said:

> *"The clinical approach to your son's perseveration will
> revolve around response cost procedures combined with
> extinction and DRO. There may be agitated stereotypical
> responses to this, which if they accelerate will lead to ex-
> tinction and time-out procedures with physical assistance
> used as needed."*

Now what parent would be willing to challenge this statement? Parents are generally alone, facing a group of professionals who all have an area of expertise. It is intimidating. I
have witnessed meetings such as this turn into opportunities
for egos to clash to see who can control the situation. A parent is outnumbered, and not privy to the jargon being tossed
around. How many parents would even know what the behavioral analyst's statements mean? In this meeting, I eventually
asked if I could translate, and this is what I described:

- We'll ignore him when he repeats himself.
- This will make him mad as hell.
- Then we'll lock him in a small room by himself, and if necessary...
- We'll drag him there.

This might sound startling, but it reflects what could happen when some theoretically designed program meets reality. Behavioral technology can be a powerful tool for positive change, and I have a lot of respect for what it can teach. But I also have seen the reality of how some "extinction programs" or "cost response procedures" will actually be run. In the description to the uninitiated, these approaches can be dressed up in clothing they do not deserve. Jargon, like some of the other problems we have considered, is just one more obstacle for a person with a disability (or for those who care about him or her) to overcome in order to take control of his or her life. The disability system has managed to infuse the control of The Godfather with its jargon, leading to: *"We'll make you an offer you can't understand."*

Let's consider Tammy, a young woman with a winning smile and lots of energy. She shares her apartment with a roommate, who also helps her with cooking, budgeting, and some other tasks. Tammy has a job in a legal office, where she helps with filing and other clerical support. She enjoys her church and the social activities of her congregation. She attends a photography class at the community college. She has a boyfriend, and she hopes to someday marry.

If this sounds like an unremarkable life, it's because it is so familiar to us. But it is not familiar to the vast majority of people with disabilities in the DIC. Tammy's IQ score, her difficulty with learning new tasks, and her occasional vulnerability to accepting people into her life whom she really doesn't know – these aren't the things that define her life.

They are important things, nonetheless, and must be supported and safeguarded. But Tammy's life is more about her dreams and desires, her participation in her community, and her hopes for the future.

I think one of the core qualities desired by the people with disabilities I have known is social belonging. By that I mean being a part of things, including something meaningful to do and a good home in a place where they can have fun with their friends and family.

Competency and Commonality

For people with disabilities to overcome the stigma of their disability and to enjoy their lives, I think there are two major areas to focus on: competency and commonality.

Competency is about being good at something. Everybody has talents. One of the keys to a successful life is to discover what your own unique talents are and to make the most of them. As you become recognized for a skill, this recognition becomes a part of your identity. For a person with a disability, this can be critical. Rather than being identified by a disability, he or she can be seen as a person who is good at something.

This talent then can be parlayed into what Wolf Wolfensberger calls a "valued social role."[44] The idea here is that if a person holds valued social roles, he or she is more likely to attain more opportunities for a better life. The theory holds that this is particularly useful for "devalued" people. One can focus on enhancing both social images and personal competencies.

Building competency is not a new idea to the DIC. Training is by and large the main focus of the system. But there is something different about competency development as I describe it. It is built on strengths, not remediation of deficits.

Commonality refers to helping people to be a part of the "typicalness" of life. When you are seen as a neighbor, a co-worker, a fellow student, a shopper, or a voter, people recognize themselves in you. As your other social roles emerge, a disability has a smaller chance to define you in some negative way. Some disability conditions, like cerebral palsy or Down Syndrome, are prominent in the life of the individual. Stressing commonality with other non-disabled people does not mean denying such a disability, or stop from taking pride in it, as some advocate. Reaching out for commonality does not mean disguising who you are.

Competencies and Person-Centered Planning

An exciting new approach to helping people discover and enhance their competencies emerged in the eighties: person-centered planning. Also termed personal futures planning, this concept moves the focus away from what the system can do to handle deficits to the individual and his or her life goals. There are many resources available on this topic, so I won't try to describe it in detail here. But one of the innovations that this process brought was a focus on each person's gifts and capacities, followed by his or her life dreams and goals.

In person-centered planning, people are not only permitted to say what their vision is for their lives, but are encouraged to. Then, building on relationships with key others, many of whom are not professionals but friends and family, the individual directs (with assistance as needed) an action plan to approach his or her dream.

Typically, the process begins with the individual with a disability hosting a meeting. He or she invites people to come and help make a future plan. Meetings are informal, often in homes or comfortable places. There is usually food and laughter. The process often begins with a "celebration" of the person's good qualities, setting a tone of possibilities from the start. There are lots of format variations for these meetings, but they usually include a discussion of dreams to achieve, nightmares to avoid, skills to apply, and needs to solve.

One of the keys of good planning is to develop a network of people who are interested in and care about the individual. This group often is called a "team" or a "circle of support." Generally, most people ask family, friends, co-workers, and other people they know from their homes and communities to participate.

An inner circle includes the people the person with a disability knows and trusts the best – intimate friends and family. The next circle includes those people he or she interacts with a lot – people he or she feels comfortable with and relies on. The last circle has those people who are also a part of the person's life, but are not as close as others.

For many people, planning will include a mixture of professionals and nonprofessionals. Agencies who assist adults with disabilities through state and federal funding are required to develop a written individualized plan for each person. This usually requires detailed planning for those areas of life where someone will need support.

Consider one parent's first experience with this process. Initially, he was not looking forward to yet another meeting on his daughter Rachel's limitations:

> *"'Futures planning, another well-intended program dreamed up in some faraway workshop,' I thought. 'Here we go again, catchy name, a warmed-over idea, fat chance.' For years, some of that same crowd had required evaluation and planning sessions that annually confirmed Rachel's limitations, and offered some degrading post-graduation training as her best hope.*

But it was not the same crowd with the same song that appeared at our home for the first of several meetings. This time Rachel was not excluded from the planning session. Encircled in her own home by her parents, her sister, her boyfriend, and her teachers, Rachel glowed through a soup and sandwich dinner and the upbeat 'planning session' that followed. She was center stage and she was loving it.

For me, it was a totally fascinating and pleasurable time, that first meeting. But more importantly, there emerged that evening the picture of a special young woman, not simply my daughter, who has a whole lot going for her. She wanted a job that would provide money for things she wanted, and she wanted a job she would enjoy. She hoped to someday be married, and to live in her own home. She was somewhat frail, but attractive, and she had a lot of native, saleable talent." [45]

No Easy Answers, but a Positive Attitude

Person-centered planning is not a magical process that provides quick answers. Sometimes it can be complicated and difficult. What Rachel feels she needs can be very different from what other people may think she needs because of their view of her disability. Or, what Rachel wants and needs may not be easily attainable, even with a lot of help. If communication is difficult, the team must project what she wants, likes, and needs and what she is trying to communicate by how she acts. Also, the people who know her best will try to share their perceptions of what she likes, wants, and needs.

Once the team has listened, learned, discussed, and documented what it knows about a person, the group members should help him or her think about some concrete directions in life. This starts with a personal futures statement. Without a clear vision of where someone is heading, it is hard for a planning team to help coordinate whatever supports the person needs.

Here is where it can get dicey, because once people find the doors are open to dream, they sometimes dream big. I have heard some of the following goals from people with significant disabilities: to be an astronaut, a pilot, a rock star, and "the boss." One person even made it clear to me that his goal was that he wanted to specifically be MY boss.

I think what typically has happened in this situation is that disability professionals, or others, dismiss these dreams as "unrealistic." How can the person with a disability possibly be a singer, a boss, an artist, or a doctor? I have watched this response crush people as they hear the refrain, "Now, Tammy, you know that isn't possible…"

But immediate rejection of someone's dreams, however seemingly impossible, denies them a way of telling people important information that should be respected. We can learn a lot from people's dreams. That doesn't mean we have to promise delivering on all of them; it just means they are worthy of respect. The proper response is to acknowledge the dream and then ask why.

Penny was a middle-aged woman with an intellectual disability who had spent her working life in a sheltered workshop. She made it clear she wanted to be a chef. She didn't want a job in any old fast food restaurant – she wanted a job in a fine restaurant where she could prepare elegant food. And to convince me, she invited me to her apartment where, she said, she would cook me a fine dinner. Not knowing what to expect, I accepted her invitation. Unfortunately, the meal was a disaster. Let me just say that her smoke detector acted as her timer, and you will get the picture.

But this didn't deter her, and I had to acknowledge how important this career goal was to her. What her person-centered planning team did was to come up with a kitchen job in a very classy restaurant. It was only salad preparation, but it turned out to be close enough for Penny.

Ultimately, she developed a close social relationship with one of the chefs who worked there. She occasionally would bring him things she baked, most of which were inedible. He thought this was hilarious. She once baked him a carrot cake, with a whole carrot baked in the middle of the cake!

Over time, the chef began working with Penny, teaching her little tricks of the trade. She began to help out regularly with desserts, and she constantly told me this was her "dream job."

Penny is not the chef she said she wanted to be. But she is darn close. And the thing to remember is that she would never have approached her career dream if people hadn't listened to her, respected what she said, and tried to help her get close to it.

Compare this to what my experience has been for most of the people I have known like Penny. Most of the time, their dreams simply were rejected as unrealistic. And if someone acknowledged their stated goals, they were first assessed and evaluated to see if they had any aptitudes or skills to fit. If those results didn't block their way, then at best they were placed in a segregated vocational training program, where they would first have to prove themselves as job-ready for their career of choice. Sadly, these environments train only to complete their available contract work, not to the interests of their participants.

Consider someone like Jessica. She uses a wheelchair and a communication board, a series of pictures representing concepts, to make her wishes known. During her person-centered planning, she expressed a desire to do professional modeling. How realistic was this for Jessica? The people helping her decided to explore the possibilities. This led to a modeling opportunity–and some pretty good money. She earned $120 an hour for the four-hour job illustrated below.

Jessica expressed her desire to model professionally, a dream that could easily have been dismissed as not practical for someone with a disability. Instead, her wish was pursued and she appeared in this ad.

Dreams are like balloons. If they can stay inflated, they can reach great heights. Unfortunately, the disability system often manages to let the air out of them. In the DIC, the typical roadblocks would have been insurmountable for Jessica and Penny to approach their dreams. Penny likely would have found herself either in a workshop training program, or if she was lucky, on a cleaning crew or in a fast food restaurant. As for Jessica, as of this writing, she no longer is looking for modeling jobs. She decided to become an artist. But her modeling experience was an important part of her career path, and she now knows to reach for the sky.

"Measuring" Life Success Can Be Misleading

Part of what drives the DIC is that it attempts to hold agencies accountable in making progress with each person

they serve. Accountability, given what we learned about places like Willowbrook where no one was watching, is not a bad
idea. It is based on each person having individual goals with
measurable objectives in a written plan.

But the first problem with so many of these plans is that
they have little connection to the real needs of the people
they are purportedly about. Instead, they are often attempts
to reach whatever the next step is in a given program curriculum, based on where people demonstrate themselves to be.
If a housing program has a checklist of cleaning skills which
must be learned, for instance, then staff there tend to view
the person through that lens. And one will likely find a cleaning goal for everyone who lives there. It is then forgotten that
someone has a burning desire to move somewhere else; the
goal is cleaning.

Sometimes the measurable objectives are almost comical,
because there is an attempt to mathematically measure some
vague or hard-to-define outcome like "integration," as in
"John will be integrated 90% of the time." How can we begin
to measure such a thing? What does it mean to be integrated?
And can we really define integration such that it has a numerical goal? Personally, and especially when I go off to our
cabin in the Ocala National Forest, there are times I prefer to
be non-integrated 100% of the time.

One of the most repeated numerical goals I have seen
relates to productivity, or what is known in the field as "on-
task" time. The objective looks like this: "Jasmine will be on-
task 95% of the time." This can be often translated as "Jasmine will do what I tell her to do." You can imagine how staff
are monitoring her every move, and marking her as attentive
to her work or not. If Jasmine isn't on-task enough, staff will
try to make her work harder, faster, and better.

This is fine unless she dislikes her work, or is tired, or maybe bored. I would hate to have someone follow me around to see exactly how on-task I am during a typical workday. Maybe what the popular literature once called Type A personalities are on-task all the time, although perhaps at the cost of their personal health.

According to a survey by *America Online* and *Salary. com*, the average worker admits to being "non-productive" 2.09 hours per eight-hour workday, not including lunch and scheduled break-time.[46] From my experience, the typical office worker spends several weeks of work time a year simply looking for things they have misplaced on their desk.

I know a lot of people who would fit this profile and who are employed at a good wage. I doubt that some of the standards we try to impose on people with disabilities would work well for us. Plus, what I have found in the real world is that productivity for a lot of people depends on who is watching them. Workers appear to work much harder when the boss is in the room.

In God We Trust, All Others Must Write Objectives

I remember once there was a big issue concerning Joan, a group home resident I was consulting about who was basically rather sloppy. (People with disabilities, while stereotyped unfairly, are not immune to annoying traits.) One particular staff member was being driven crazy by Joan's dirty laundry, unwashed dishes, and careless ways. This behavior can indeed be a problem in a communal house such as a group home, as it impacts everyone who lives there. It seemed to me that this home arrangement was a particularly bad match for Joan. But the staff person was determined instead to get her to change, and he began to implement some rules and pretty intense consequences for sloppy housekeeping.

This eventually caused a number of difficult and unnecessary struggles as Joan first resisted, then got angry, then tried to avoid the situation through some devious means. The whole thing escalated into a crisis that wasn't necessary. It turned into a struggle to determine who was in charge, Joan or the house manager.

Ultimately the team managed to work with Joan in a more respectful way to maintain a basic hygienic level of living, while helping her to find a place where she did not have to worry if her bedroom was untidy. But the thing that most amazed me was what I saw when I gave one of the residential staff a ride to a meeting about Joan. Stopping by his house to pick him up, I saw that his apartment was in incredible disarray. I wondered how he would have felt if his boss put a housekeeping goal in his evaluation, and sent someone over to collect data on whether he had done his dishes. Or what his reaction would be if given an ultimatum by someone he didn't choose who was paid to look after him.

I once saw a hygiene goal that made me laugh out loud. It read: "Bob will learn to shave 75% of his face with 90% accuracy." Apparently the staff had decided to take shaving a step at a time, and getting the whole face right was just too hard for Bob. Hard to imagine how this one was done, but I doubt Bob would want or need to measure it. Teach me if I can learn to master this, or help me if I can't, but don't spend time counting how many hairs I have left on my right side.

It seems to me that many programs just attach a number to an objective to make it seem measurable. "Look, we can count this and we have data." But often the data has no real meaning. I have seen so many useless goals in my career. "Jan will use the crosswalk with 80% accuracy." What does this mean? Apparently, Jan can get hit by a car a couple of times and still meet her objective.

My favorite learning objective of all time was one that said: "Carl will use the toilet with 100% accuracy." Poor Carl and how unfair. Ask any woman, and she will tell you it is probably impossible for any man to use the toilet with 100% accuracy. One had to wonder if the staff had a toilet bowl that had a bull's eye, and if they awarded Carl points for accuracy. I imagine that if they could, the staff at this agency would probably assign new disability labels to the people in their toilet-accuracy-training program. I can picture "over-achievers," and "underachievers," as well as other disability labels as illustrated below.

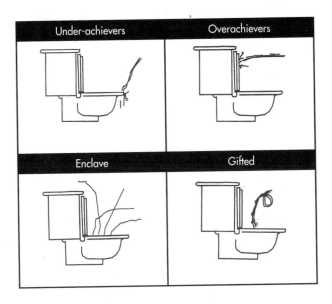

Good Planning vs. Bad Planning

Planning can be a liberating experience. Good planning can open doors of possibility and forge new connections to places and people for the individual with a disability. Or, planning can focus on deficits, be dominated by professionals, and end up directing the person to a life of segregation and training. And sometimes it is somewhere in between. Most importantly, the plan itself is only a plan. It is what happens as a result of planning that really counts. Being happy with a nicely written service plan is much like saying a restaurant is good because it has a nice menu. Better taste the food first.

Here is my list of a few "red flags" for someone who is evaluating the effectiveness of planning meetings and the resulting set of goals and objectives. If these things have happened to you or someone you care about, I would suggest you try to find some people who understand person-centered planning and try again.

Bad planning for people with disabilities occurs when:
- the people planning do not fully understand who you are and what you want,
- the people planning make decisions for you,
- you do not understand what advice is being given to you,
- you are not given choices about what you want,
- you are not comfortable with the location where planning will take place,
- you did not choose who would be present for the planning,
- a planning meeting is not convenient in time or place,
- the planning document does not reflect your wishes or what was agreed to at the meeting, or
- the planning document is restrictive or talks about you in an impersonal way.

Social Glue, Granfalloons, and Natural Supports

From recognition, as long as it does not threaten us, comes comfort. We are more open to others when we identify a commonality. A core quality of social belonging is to express our humanity through things that are commonly known and accepted. These can be very simple things, such as our language, the roles we have, our dress, the things we do for fun, and our interests.

Our commonalities are what I call "social glue." What we share in common often forms the basis of many of our relationships – they are the things that bind us together. Social psychologists have found that one of the most predictive factors in the development of some social relationships is simply physical proximity – being in the same approximate physical space over time. This is a powerful reason why people with disabilities should not be physically segregated from others in society. Without proximity, there is much less likelihood of social connections. Their relationships become limited to those around them, who are primarily other people with the same type of disability.

But proximity alone is not sufficient for relationships. There need to be elements of commonality for social glue to work.

Kurt Vonnegut, in his masterful book *Cat's Cradle*,[47] talks about people feeling a sense of belonging to a group that really has little meaning. He calls this a "granfalloon," summarizing the idea with the line: "If you wish to study a granfalloon, just remove the skin of a toy balloon." But the interesting thing about a granfalloon is that it illustrates how important social connections can form, despite their lack of any deep underlying commonality. An example of a granfalloon happened to me one day while I was shopping along the main street in my then-home town of Keene, New Hampshire. I

saw a man my age wearing a New York Giants (football) shirt.
I happened to have on a hat with the same logo. Based on the
simple clothing messages we were wearing, we struck up an
animated conversation.

What did we have in common besides wearing the same
logo of a sports team? Actually, aside from our opinions about
the chances of our team for the year, we had very little else in
common. But I enjoyed his personality. This is how relationships form. It often doesn't take much, but it does take something to break through the wall of anonymity with which we
surround ourselves. I easily spent a couple of hours at the local bar talking and having a beer with this guy I didn't really
know.

We Seem to Need to Categorize People

Social grouping experiments by Henri Tajfel in the early
seventies demonstrated that the very act of artificially cat-
egorizing people into groups is enough to develop coherent
social identities. Tajfel's studies show that strangers form
groups in which they treat each other as allies or close friends
based on insignificant criteria that he randomly assigned.

In the experiment, sixty-four boys, fourteen and fifteen
years old, were told that they were to estimate a series of
varying numbers of dots presented on a screen. After the esti-
mates, the boys were told that they were going to be grouped.
In one group, the boys were labeled as either "overestimat-
ers" or "underestimaters," and in the other, they were labeled
as "accurate" or "less accurate." They were actually assigned
to groups at random (their social glue was basically imposed).
They then were asked to give rewards and penalties in real
money to others, not knowing their identity, only the label of
the recipients.

Tajfel found that when choosing between two boys in the same group, no matter what the label, choices were generally made based on fairness. But when the choice was between one boy in their "in-group" and one boy in their "out-group" the boys discriminated in favor of the "in-group."

What seems to happen is that people immediately look for and bond with those who are part of their new "in-group," while seeking to protect themselves from those in the "out-group." Just having membership in a group, even if it is assigned and is based on something inconsequential, seems to make people think that their group must be the best group for them.[48]

This group identity phenomenon makes it all the more challenging for those who are not in the "in-group." For people with significant disabilities, the wall of anonymity is much higher because of stereotypes, uncertainties, and other barriers to communication and connectivity.

But a commonality really can help overcome the wall, even if it is only a surface quality. How often have you driven in a far-off state, only to see a car go by with the same license plate that you have? The urge to look in at the passengers in the car is powerful. We muse, "I wonder if I know them?" Of course, the chances of that are generally miniscule, but that doesn't deter us. I once watched my neighbors at a campsite cement a bond simply because they both took the same exit off the Garden State Parkway in New Jersey to get home. Ah, the stuff friendships are made of. This kind of thing happens all the time. The commonality may be only a license plate, but it can be enough to generate a conversation. And once you converse, you begin to share history, and even friendship. A new in-group is formed with the social glue.

Even our technology can be the starting point of a relationship. People with iPods who happen to sit next to each other on a plane, bus, or train often will compare their music. I happen to use another Apple product, one of their laptop computers. At the time of this writing, Apple has less than five percent of market share for personal computers, making Apple users unique enough to be a sort of club. And so, when another Apple user notices my laptop, he or she will often make some sort of comment, often leading to a conversation.

Regarding the application of these concepts to people with disabilities, Jan Nisbet and David Hagner at the University of New Hampshire in 1988 first mentioned in the disability literature the idea of using supports that are more common to everyday community environments. They termed these approaches "natural supports."[49] Subsequent research pointed out a number of problems with how the disability service system was supporting people with disabilities in the workplace, including using training, jargon, and other approaches that were intrusive to the work environment. An artificial, more professionalized type of approach had the result of socially isolating the worker with a disability, and getting in the way of more natural methods of support from co-workers and others.

What I believe this means for people with disabilities is that, if we can help them express their interests, experiences, and personalities, their commonalities with people will be easier to determine. Thus, two different things should be part of our services for people with disabilities. We should:

- minimize the things that are atypical and do not fit the norms and expectations of the culture, and
- maximize those things that do meet the expectations of the culture the individual wishes to be a part of.

Let's take these one at a time.

Standing Out or Fitting In

Minimizing what is atypical about people involves helping them not to appear too abnormal. Of course there is no good way to define what normal is. But what I mean is to support people to learn to act and appear culturally acceptable. I don't mean anyone should try to hide one's disability. Nor do I wish people to suppress their unique personalities. But many people with little social experience do not understand that something like bad hygiene has a social cost, as do certain kinds of behavior. And just as important, I also think we need to take a hard look at the artificial qualities of many disability services and the artifacts of those services that surround people.

For example, I discussed in Chapter Four the example of Theresa, who worked at a restaurant and was made to wear "smile stickers" for good behavior. When she obtained five, she was allowed to buy a soda for break. When I visited her workplace and was introduced to her, and I noticed she had four smile stickers on her shirt. I asked her about it, and she said "One more and I earn Coke for break."

The person supporting her said this approach was generally keeping Theresa from misbehaving. But I wondered at what cost. No one else was wearing smile stickers (this was not Wal-Mart, after all), and no one else was interacting with her at the restaurant. When I ordered lunch, I asked the waitress why Theresa was wearing so many smile stickers. She shrugged and said, "I'm not really sure – some sort of program they've got her on."

While Theresa's behaviors could be atypical and could be a barrier for her social acceptance at work, it seemed to me the solution was just as bad. The people helping her had exaggerated her disability. They had reduced her "misbehaviors," but also had further made Theresa different from everyone else. She not only had a program, she had it advertised on her shirt. The other workers took their breaks based on how long they had worked. Theresa got to take hers when she had earned enough stickers. This created a mystique about Theresa that made her seem not "one of us."

I have witnessed various behavior programs, teaching programs, and support systems for people with disabilities where the only thought is "will this work?" There is little regard as to what it looks like to someone else. The social perception of our program efforts in community settings is absolutely critical for people with disabilities. If social belonging is indeed a core need, then we must begin to pay more attention to this.

People with disabilities certainly have needs that often require a solution that is atypical. From wheelchairs to assistive technology, from extra training to help with self-care, disability professionals often are faced with how to solve support problems.

One key factor in this challenge is to *minimize obtrusiveness*, and the other is to seek solutions that will be *naturally valid*. Natural validity is the extent to which something is acceptable to the cultural norms of a setting. Every setting tends to evolve its own unique set of expectations for behavior. When these expectations are violated, the individual is at risk of being socially ostracized by the other members of the setting. When they are met, the individual is more likely to be perceived as being "one of us." Historically, we have ignored the concept of natural validity. In fact, providing supports that are sensitive to the social expectations of the setting the individual with a disabilities is in should be the "default setting" for all of our supports.

Wait Your Turn

Ronald was a young man with Down Syndrome who had just landed his first job as a grounds assistant at his local YMCA. Enthusiastic by nature, he would be so excited to cash his paycheck that as soon as he got it, he would walk directly from work to his bank and head straight for a teller. If someone was already at the window, he would wait behind for his turn, like he was taught by his teacher. The only problem was, the bank had a single waiting line for all the tellers about six feet removed from the teller counter, and Ronald was jumping ahead of everyone in it.

In the small community where he lived, this became a major issue. People would get mad at him for being so rude, but he was simply unaware. It was only when he was observed at the bank by a neighbor who took him aside to explain how this particular bank handled "waiting for your turn" that the situation was resolved.

Fitting in also requires adhering to a set of expectations sometimes. For example, there are sets of expected behaviors in a movie theatre, food store, bank, or a restaurant. Certainly work environments also have behavioral expectations. If you violate those expectations, you likely will not be welcomed in those environments by others who frequent them.

Many people with disabilities have no experience with these sometimes bewildering sets of community standards, and so can violate them without even knowing it. I believe a key cornerstone to community services is to help people learn these often unwritten rules of behavior. It sometimes can be far more important to teach citizens with disabilities cultural norms than anything else.

Self Expression: Is That Your Dog?

Many people with disabilities have little experience in the rich life that community offers. I sadly have known far too many people who have never explored many activities to see if they even like doing them: taking pictures, going to concerts or movies, creating art, playing music. If we can help people explore their environment and then find out what makes them happy, motivated, or involved, we can help them to be a part of the world. And once they are a part of a community based not on their disabilities, but on their interests, we help them to express their desires.

How do we express our interests? There are lots of ways. Consider the space we live or work in. We often display things that are a part of our lives. Look at your desk. Most people have photographs of people, pets, or places they love, or symbols of accomplishments or passions. There might be a coffee mug that says "Gone Fishing" or a golf trophy. These kinds of symbols are just one example of self-expression. Our conversations, how we are introduced, the friends we have, even the clothes we wear, can all help us connect with others through a commonality.

One of the most direct routes to commonality and social connections is through the social roles people have. John McKnight and John Kretzman, co-directors of Community Studies at the Institute for Policy Research at Northwestern University, have studied how the assets of a community can be used to help the more vulnerable members of that community.[50] Membership in community associations, for example, can offer people with disabilities a valued role as well as a way to access diverse individuals with whom to interact. Helping people with disabilities join the Rotary, garden club, the community choir, or other such groups can help them be a stronger part of their community.

There are, of course, many other social roles beyond associational membership. Being a homeowner, shopper, churchgoer, gardener, or pet owner can help establish an identity beyond "person with a disability." People who share these roles have common interests to talk about. Or they might have common needs to address, like finding a ride to church or picking out the right tomatoes to plant. These concerns can become the basis for relationships.

Sometimes social connections can occur by simply showing up at a place at predictable times. Being a Friday regular at the community diner can lead to a sense of social belonging, if those who are there are open to accepting you. While presence is important, so is "fitting in" with dress, customs, and other features of the group.

In fact, I believe that "acting as a bridge" to fitting in is a critical role for disability professionals. For far too long, disability professionals have acted only as caretakers, helping respond to the needs of people with disabilities. Certainly there is a place to offer caretaking to people with significant needs. But I think the system has displaced existing natural community-based possibilities that could solve some of the concerns.

Sometimes it is the simple things we can help people to do that can make all the difference. I once asked a residential staff person to help Bonnie, one of the individuals with disabilities we supported, to take a picture of her pet dog. We told Bonnie that she should keep this picture in her purse in case she wanted to show it to a new friend. It turned out that showing this picture to others was the start of at least two new friendships for her, based on a shared love of dogs.

The more people can express their interests and passions, whether they be about a hobby, a career, a sports team, music, a television show, or the movies, the more likely they will be able to connect with others who share their interests. We should help people learn how to apply some social glue.

Out of the Cold

By 1990, my disability consulting was taking me beyond New England. I had gotten pretty good at helping to get people with significant disabilities out of the workshop and day programs and find them real jobs in the community. Dawn (who now had a busy career in public relations for non-profits) and I made a decision to start a new publication together. It was to be a newsletter addressing the employment of people with disabilities, and we called it *InfoLines*. We purchased a Mac Plus computer and began producing and marketing *InfoLines* all over the country. We immediately acquired a relatively small but dedicated following. Many of our original subscribers from those first years have remained with us over the nearly twenty years we have produced it.

It was at this time that we made a major change in our lives. We decided to leave New Hampshire. Although Dawn and I loved the area and its natural beauty, the winters were becoming increasingly hard for us to negotiate. I sometimes felt our home life was an endless series of chores to either get ready for winter or deal with the snow and cold itself. Our last winter in New Hampshire was particularly harsh. One morning was so cold that when I got into my car and went to adjust the rear-view mirror, it simply snapped off in my hand.

I still remember the moment I knew I needed to move. I had just finished shoveling my driveway. Reaching the road, I turned to survey my accomplishment. At that moment, a monumental ledge of snow and ice slid from the roof of our garage, right onto the clean driveway I had just finished. Looking on in shock, I didn't even try to start again. I climbed over the snow and went inside. Dawn looked at my face and said, "What's the matter?"

I just vacantly stared ahead and asked. "Honey, what is your favorite warm state?"

"A hot bath on a cold winter night?" she answered.

"No, not a state of being," I replied. "A state – like the kind you move to."

My never-ending winter task of shoveling snow in New Hampshire

We soon decided to move to a lovely town in Florida called St. Augustine, the nation's "oldest city," the first permanent European settlement in the US. We visited there and, while walking through a quiet historic neighborhood, we came upon a man working hard fixing up a small bungalow. Dawn immediately feel in love with the house and its view of a small inlet in the backyard, and I was taken with its possibilities as well. After striking up a conversation (using our "commonalities" as a starting point), we learned that he was the owner of the house, and that he planned to put it up for sale. We struck a deal then and there.

While I left many of my work contacts behind, my national consulting had grown considerably, so it really did not matter where I was based. And Dawn was ready for a change as well. Fifteen years later, we still live in that same house, although we have expanded it in both size and scope. We have welcomed with great joy a child, and have added friends, work colleagues, and new activities to this place we call "home."

Dawn and I are very active in our neighborhood and community, and we know firsthand how our social roles enhance quality of life. I helped found St. Augustine's first Neighborhood Council and served as its president. We also have been active in other community affairs, such as historic preservation, educational functions, and local political campaigns.

But my work to open doors for people with disabilities still is my passion. And in my work, I have a sense of who I am and what my place is in the world – something sadly missing for too many people with disabilities today.

Pictured are, from left to right, St. Augustine Mayor George Gardner, Florida Secretary of State Glenda Hood, Citizens for the Preservation of St. Augustine board member Nancy Sikes-Kline, and myself, the President of the Neighborhood Council of St. Augustine in 2004.

CHAPTER SEVEN

People Need Jobs,
Not Day Programs

*"Far too many thousands of citizens with disabilities
who progressed through school systems receiving special education and related services are not enjoying
integrated or productive post-school lives. They were
not functioning in real jobs in the real world for
at least minimum wages and employer provided benefits when they exited school, nor are they now."*

– Lou Brown

When I ask people in my seminars why they work, the
number one answer is always "money."

There is no question that our wages are important to our
quality of life. And our culture has an expectation for people
to be productive, get paid what they are worth, and make
their own way. Certainly this is also true for people with disabilities, probably the most impoverished minority group in
the U.S. As a group, they often live on below-poverty level income. Among working adults, nearly 40% of people with disabilities have family incomes less than 200% of the poverty
level.[51]

But work is not simply about money for many of us. It
certainly cannot be for those paid so poorly in human services, or they must be very bad judges about their career choice!
Beyond survival, work always has been a means for status,

self-definition, and personal accomplishment. Work defines us. It gives us meaning. It is a major part of our social lives. Almost half of our waking lives is spent with our co-workers – a scary thought for some of us.

People who work use their employment as one of their social roles. In fact, one of the first things we seek when meeting someone new is to find out what they do. We use this information, along with other social cues, behavior, and professed interests, to "size up" the individual. Our job is like a membership card that tells people we belong: "Here I am, and this is what I do."

Interestingly, professionals who work in the DIC often get a curious response when they explain that they work with people with disabilities. Responses can range from "Good for you! You must be so patient," to "Thank God there are people like you; how do you do it?"

It seems that people who work with people who have disabilities are stereotyped themselves as having remarkable patience and saint-like qualities. These stereotypes are based on assumptions about needing these qualities in order to work with people assumed to be difficult to work with, slow learners with challenging behavior, and so on.

I certainly have worked with people who fit this profile, but they were hardly limited to people with disabilities. These kind of challenges occur with all kinds of people. Patience is a virtue we can all use, in any line of work. Yet far too few of us exhibit it. I find the saintly characteristic sometimes awarded to me because of my line of work to be pretty ironic. Dawn believes I am often the least patient person on earth. I often express my frustration waiting in any line, whether at the bank or at a toll both.

Stereotyping also happens in other occupations. Accountants are often assumed to be precise and unexciting. Artists can be prejudged as temperamental. But these kinds of characterizations are minor compared to the negative assumptions made about someone who is unemployed. In our culture, we expect people pull to "pull their own weight." Those who don't are at risk of being considered incompetent or lazy. These are not labels someone with a disability, already at risk of negative stereotypes, can afford.

Just having a job gives someone a basic level of status. A job title or career that is valued gives even more. For someone who has been labeled with a disability, a job can be one of the most important paths to a quality life. This reflects the high cultural value our society gives to work. Generally, people tend to prize productivity, accomplishment, competence, and financial success. We signify this by how we recognize someone's career success socially. Along with recognition come various status symbols, including possessions, prestige, power, control, and influence.

So people with disabilities are faced with a true challenge. Considered unproductive and often undesirable, they are not generally welcomed to the workplace. Yet, work is one of the primary and expected ways they can define themselves beyond their disabilities. And the wages from work are key tools in pursuing a quality life and expressing success and status.

The DIC response to this challenge has been twofold:

1. to develop a work readiness training system, in order to make people more employable, and
2. to provide work in a sheltered place where people with disabilities would not have to face the demands of competitive economics.

As we have seen, neither of these approaches has been effective. In fact, their results are abysmal. People with disabilities rarely reach the magic state of "employable." And the segregation to which they are subjected further defines them by their disability rather than their employability.

Supported Employment

In the early 1980s, after years of no improvement in the employment rate for people with significant disabilities, researchers tested a new notion. What if people need not go through the "flow-through" service continuum in order to be employable? This approach, called supported employment, changed the core belief that people must be trained in work readiness before they were employed ("train, then place"). Instead, it stated that people with disabilities should get right to work, with as much help for as long as needed to support them to learn their jobs ("place, then train and support").

I was still in New Hampshire at the time this idea took root, and the more people we helped get to work through supported employment, the more I was convinced that this was possible for far more people than anyone previously believed. Not only that, it seemed to be one of the gateways to a whole host of other successes in life. People changed when they had real jobs in real businesses that they liked. People whom we had difficulty teaching about hygiene started to clean themselves up. People who had not cared about their appearance starting choosing their clothes more carefully. Self-esteem, confidence, and a positive outlook seemed to improve.

After relocating to Florida, I began to focus more and more on advocating for people whom the field had traditionally called "unemployable" to get jobs. Dawn and I continued to publish *InfoLines*, and we started a publishing company that offered resources on community inclusion for people with disabilities, particularly in the area of employment. Meanwhile, my consulting and training services were taking me all over the country. I was elected to the board of a new organization, the Association for Persons in Supported Employment, and later became its board president. I was soon asked to speak on employment at conferences outside the US, including Canada, Norway, and Spain.

I think the reason I was becoming so busy was that there was a growing understanding that people with disabilities have by far the highest unemployment rate of any other minority group. And they face numerous obstacles to getting a job, including discrimination so pervasive that in 1990 the U.S. Congress finally passed a law addressing it, the Americans with Disabilities Act.

Most People Are Forced to Waste Time

In 1999, I became involved in a class action lawsuit that had been going on for some time against the state of Florida. Called *Prado-Steiman v. Bush*, it was filed by attorneys representing people with developmental disabilities who had been denied services for which they were eligible. Ultimately, the case was settled. The settlement required the state to provide adequate funding for a variety of services for people who want to live at home or in other community settings.[52]

My role was as an expert witness regarding the employment of people with developmental disabilities in the state. I visited five individuals in different locations; I observed their day programs, met with and interviewed each person and their families, and reviewed their files. I then revisited them almost a year later to see how far they had come. It was discouraging. I will briefly share the stories of two of the people I saw, because they represent so many others.

Joan

I visited Joan in her apartment. A twenty-five-year-old woman with cerebral palsy, Joan lived with her sixty-six-year-old mother, who supported her daily activities. Joan used a motorized wheelchair. She was bi-lingual and bright, and had a high level of communication skills. She was able to do math, count money, make change, and use a phone. She wrote poetry, and she said she was bored and lonely. Her mother said she was attending classes to receive her GED. Her interests included music, shopping for clothes, jewelry, and make-up.

Joan told me she had been asking for a job for over two years. She wished to be a translator or counselor, preferably working with young children. She said she also would be interested in working in an office, where she could file, do word processing, and answer phones. At one time she volunteered at a medical facility, talking to patients, delivering medications, and doing errands for nurses.

After being on a waiting list for some time, she attended a sheltered workshop, where she did some assembly tasks. She did not receive any meaningful pay, earning two to three dollars per *week*. (No, that low salary is not a typo.) According to case notes I reviewed, Joan still was considered in need of training to be eligible for supported employment. I did not agree with this judgment. In actuality, Joan had many strengths and capabilities. She should have been working in a job related to her skills and interests a long time ago.

Donald

When I first met Donald, he was unemployed, and I was struck by his eagerness to go to work. On our first meeting, he looked me up and down and said, "So, will *you* get me a job?"

He was thirty-four years old and labeled with mild mental retardation and muscle weakness on the right side. He lived with his parents. He spent his days in a workshop where there was infrequent work. His parents reaffirmed to me that he wanted a community job, something they had been saying to disability professionals for quite some time.

Donald's annual support plan at that time documented several of his wishes, including a job at Blockbuster Video or in a music-related setting, both of which he repeated to me. Donald also expressed interest in working with animals, a desire to learn how to cook, and a preference to be around lots of people and activity. He also enjoyed working on a computer.

Later, I returned to see what had happened for Donald and his work hopes. I was directed to see him working at his new job, which was as a janitor in an enclave at an air force base. As discussed in Chapter Two, an enclave is a work model in which a group of people with disabilities work together. The workers are not employees of the host employer; they receive paychecks from the agency. At the air force base, the agency employees had their own "operations center," which was a separate room in a separate building on the base, and their own uniforms, labeled with the agency's name.

Donald worked with twelve other individuals with disabilities under the supervision of three agency supervisors. The enclave, along with the placement of approximately sixty-five other people with disabilities, was through the National Industries for the Severely Handicapped (NISH), a government "set-aside" work program for people with disabilities.

Donald had been bored with his lack of meaningful work in a sheltered workshop for a long time. He clearly had strong preferences and dreams for his life, and he wished to be busy. But Donald worked in the enclave only three days a week, and averaged only about eight paid hours each week. Even then, his family reported there were days he could not attend "the job" (as opposed to "his job"), because they believed the agency wanted to provide other people with disabilities that they served with an opportunity to work.

One feature of a real job in supported employment is that the job belongs to the individual, who is supervised by an employer, and not under the control of the support agency. Donald, however, appeared to be an interchangeable worker within a general job contract at the base, with little say as to his hours or days. According to his family, this situation made them uneasy and unwilling to complain, for fear of further limiting his access to the little paid work he had.

I watched Donald generally do a good job with his cleaning tasks. He worked dutifully, although his job coach gave him numerous cues to remind him about steps he had missed in a task or about not completing the task to a quality level. When I asked about the likelihood of Donald moving to a community job that was more individualized, I was told it was still unlikely, due to transportation as well as his "non-readiness" due to "task completion issues."

Once again, the reason given for a person with a disability not accessing real life in the community was some label based on performance not meeting an arbitrary standard. But Donald's performance was not being fairly assessed in a job that had little connection to his interests. Despite this, I felt Donald performed quite well and was just in need of better training in order for him to perform better. Rather than relying on ongoing verbal direction from a job coach, he would benefit from a more systematic approach. More troubling, however, was the lack of social integration for Donald, as well as the other individuals from the agency. One of the primary goals of supported employment is individualization and social integration with people without disabilities.

I thought Donald would benefit greatly from being around a variety of people and in a field related to his interests. In my time observing Donald on the job, I did not see any social interaction between non-disabled base employees and the workers with disabilities. Social isolation for people with disabilities is often related to the stigma the individual carries. These workers did not appear to be employees of the base, but were clearly a segregated, contracted unit. Also, disability advocates have strongly and rightfully criticized the overuse of cleaning work for people with disabilities despite their diverse interests and skills.

The agency repeatedly stated it found individualized job development to be difficult for Donald because the agency could not provide transportation from his home or the center to a community job site. This limited the job opportunities to locations close to his home so that "the parents could provide transportation." But transportation should be a part of the supports Donald receives. Indeed, it is essential to a system that is individualized and integrated within a community.

Although his wages had improved, Donald's job situation continued to be inadequate, leaving him still unchallenged, socially isolated, and with far too few hours. He had many skills and interests that could make him a valuable employee to many local businesses. Yet he still had practically no situational job exposure other than this very part-time cleaning work, limiting his knowledge of what potential jobs were available, and what he might enjoy and be proficient at. His ability to make an informed choice about his own future continued to be severely limited by the service system's failure to provide him integrated work experiences.

Joan and Donald are just two of the many people who are frustrated by wasting their lives in programs that are not coming close to helping them reach their potential. Every place I visited, then and since, whether it was a day program or a sheltered workshop, there were too many people sitting around with nothing much to do. And even in those places that are busy, people with disabilities are working on things that they generally have little interest in doing, grouped with other people who share their disability.

It was the late Joseph Bauer, the parent of a young man with an intellectual disability that I had come to know while living in New Hampshire, who said it best. His family's story is told in *Part of the Community*, by my colleagues who still work at the Institute on Disability at the University of New Hampshire. Joseph said, "We found out quickly that the term sheltered workshop glosses over the reality of what it is – total segregation and the daily death of the soul."[53]

Artie Sings Commercials for Free

There were nearly 500,000 people with developmental disabilities in various day programs throughout the U.S. in 2002; the number is surely larger now.[54] About three out of four are in segregated programs.[55] These are people waiting to do something meaningful and be paid for it. They have autism, or intellectual disabilities, or some other label, and perhaps a variety of physical and sensory disabilities. They are people like Artie, who has autism. It has taken me years to learn that we often just have to ignore what so many evaluators have decided – that people like Artie are unemployable.

"Ohh, I wish I were an Oscar Mayer wiener..."

Artie loved to sing. Some people sing in the car when they are by themselves. Other people sing opera in the shower, or karaoke at a bar. Artie sang everywhere. Most of us have certain songs we like to sing – maybe a popular song from our past, or something currently being played on the radio. For Artie, it was commercials, especially the older ones he'd heard on the radio or television when he was younger.

"Schaefer is the one beer to have, when you're having more than one..."

Artie was a thin, angular man in his fifties with piercing eyes and a booming voice. The airwaves were filled with advertisements, and it seemed that Artie knew them all.

"Join the Pepsi generation..."

Artie had been institutionalized at an early age. He was tested and labeled as "autistic." He kept to himself, rarely looked at anyone directly, and moved in unusual ways over and over. As I mentioned earlier, experts call this perseveration, and consider it one of the identifying traits of autism. Of course, if repeating things over and over was considered to be a major disability, most of us know plenty of our own relatives who would fit the label.

But what was great about Artie was that not only was he an encyclopedia of commercials, but we never knew when he would belt one out. If he got tired, or bored, or frustrated, he would sing. When Artie finally left the institution, he moved to a small apartment with a roster of paid staff who helped him. He attended a program designed to help people work and earn income. Artie had no job experiences, so the program staff decided to hold a meeting. With Artie's permission, they invited into his living room his family, friends, and the staff who knew him best.

The meeting was fun, and everyone learned a lot. The most surprising thing the staff learned that evening was that Artie could type. He was actually quite fast. They tried him on a computer, and he whizzed through whatever they gave him.

"Hey, Artie, you're so fast we'll have to give you a seat belt," someone joked.

"Seat belt, nothing, let's install an air bag in the computer," chimed in someone else.

Artie didn't respond to the teasing, but kept on typing. After a search of local employers, Tom, the staff member assigned to Artie, found an employer who needed someone right away. The company was a small business that processed charge card invoices into a database. Artie would be typing for a living. The professional staff who supported Artie gathered to discuss how to introduce Artie to the company workplace. The conversation proceeded something like this:

"Should they know he's autistic?"

"Why should they? That won't tell anything about Artie, really. It'll probably just scare them."

"Well, how should we explain the singing?"

"Let's just tell them he likes to sing."

And that's exactly what happened. Artie was introduced like any other new employee. The supervisor, Mr. Meyers, took him around. They leisurely made their way through the one large, open room, with computer stations on each wall.

"Hey, Bob, this is the new guy Artie."

"Hi, Mr. Meyers. Hey, Artie, welcome to computer land."

Artie looked away and said nothing.

"Artie's kinda shy, Bob, and he usually doesn't say much. If you're lucky, though, he just might sing you a song."

"Oh yeah? That should be interesting."

So no one made a big deal about Artie's "perseveration" and "autism." The staff knew from experience that the labels would make people wary. And although his co-workers noticed how Artie would repeat doing things, or how he looked away when someone looked at him, they also noticed he was a fast worker, and that he seemed to really love doing his job. But what really got their attention happened on Artie's first day. After typing in data for about an hour, Artie paused, stretched, and sang, *"Call Roto-Rooter, that's the name, and away go troubles down the drain..."*

Everyone stopped. All eyes were on Artie. He let the last note ring out. Then, it was like magic. Everyone clapped! People laughed. His co-workers took a collective breath, and went back to work. The program staff thought all would be fine. And, in fact, things seemed to go along quite smoothly for a couple of weeks. Then came a phone call from Artie's supervisor to the agency staff member who supported Artie:

"Tom? This is Al Meyers, Artie's boss."

"Good morning, Al. Everything OK? How's Artie?"

"Oh, Artie's just fine. Doing a great job."

"That's great. What can I do for you?"

"Well, we have a bit of a problem – seems I have a room full of people singing commercials."

Tom didn't quite know what to say, so he agreed he should come right over. He was expecting the worst. On the drive to meet with Mr. Meyers, he even figured there was a good chance Artie would be fired. When he arrived, Mr. Meyers waved him inside. Tom sat down anxiously, waiting for bad news. Mr. Meyers had pulled out the productivity counts for the past month.

"Well, Tom, to be honest, I don't understand it."

"Understand what, Mr. Meyers?"

"These numbers. The people in Artie's department are singing away, yet productivity hasn't gone down at all. In fact, it's gone up."

"Well," said Tom, uncertainly, "that's great."

Tom then looked at his watch and said, "It's almost break time, isn't it? Would you mind if we go ask people about what's going on?"

And so Tom and Mr. Meyers went out into the data entry floor to talk to some of the workers. The first thing they heard was laughter. Then,

"N-E-S-T-L-E-S, Nestles makes the very best–chocolate!"

According to the workers, Artie's singing was just what they needed. Data entry can be boring. The repetitive motion, in fact, can even lead to physical problems, such as carpal tunnel syndrome. One worker said it best:

"Hey, thanks to Artie, now when we get tired, we stop, we stretch, we sing a commercial, and we go back to work! It's great!"

Mr. Meyers just shook his head. But why argue with success? Productivity was up, and so was morale. He hadn't anticipated this when he hired Artie, but then, Artie had brought something to his workplace. And remarkably enough, it was something that Artie's disability professionals had spent years trying to eliminate. It seems Artie had something of value for his co-workers, and his co-workers had helped Artie come out of his own world a bit, too.

Everyone Is Employable

Joan, Donald, Artie – and the many others sitting in day programs – are waiting to be deemed "ready to work," when they should be working NOW.

They should be making a decent wage and paying taxes.

They should be out in the world with our support, making friends and learning new skills.

My experience has found these statements to be true, regardless of the disability.

But there is one group of individuals with disabilities that has had a particularly challenging time getting past stereotypes to get into the workforce – people with serious mental illness. While requiring different and unique support needs

than those with developmental disabilities such as intellectual disabilities or autism, these individuals have really been left
behind in the work world. Employment rates for people who
reported serious mental illness range only from 32% to 61%.
Among those with serious mental illness who had schizo-
phrenia and related disorders, employment rates ranged from
22% to 40%.[56] Individuals with psychiatric disabilities also
have the lowest employment outcomes of any other disability
group served in state and/or federal programs.[57]

These statistics are particularly discouraging in light of
the studies that show that work can improve the recovery of
those with mental illness. Employment has been found to
be important, not only because of the direct improvements
in activity, social contacts, and wages, but also because work
may promote gains in related areas such as self-esteem, integration into the community, and quality of life.[58]

Work also may decrease the use of mental health services
and reliance on the mental health system.[59] In a 2000 study,
people with mental illness who had community jobs felt their
work enabled a shift from "pathology to productivity" and a
development of self-worth and life satisfaction. The individuals in this study described improved mental health and self-
esteem and a more integrated, "normalized" way of life.[60] The
long-term effects of employment for people with mental illness also are beneficial. One study found a reduction of hos-
pitalization rates that was maintained many years after employment.[61]

Despite these promising findings, the fact is that people
with mental illness probably face some of the strongest discrimination when it comes to getting a job. Of all the disability labels, mental illness seems to provoke the strongest tendency to negatively characterize the individual and elicits the
most fear and concern. And this is yet one more reason why

the disability system must work better to promote the capacities of each potential worker with a disability, without labels and jargon, one person at a time.

Acceptance of Behaviors at Work Depends on Context

In my experience, employer discrimination, while a major issue, is only a part of the battle. What really keeps people out of employment is often the DIC itself. Because the system is so attuned to deficits and their remediation, staff have historically often rejected out-of-hand the notion that a person with a significant disability can work. I know this because in my past, my agency did it, too.

Danny was a young man who had been labeled with both a psychiatric disorder and an intellectual disability. He had worked at a sheltered workshop for years. Tall and lanky, he walked with a John Wayne strut. But the first thing people described about Danny was the fact that he was a world-class spitter. Most people find spitting somewhat gross. When we see someone spit, we generally find it disgusting. And when we see someone spit indoors, it is really disgusting.

But neither of these sights compares to the experience of being hit with spit. At the end of the baseball season of 1996, Baltimore Orioles second baseman Roberto Alomar spit at an umpire who called him out on strikes. The video image of Alomar spitting in the face of the umpire caused a public outcry unusual in its support of the umpire, usually the object of derision by many a baseball fan. Even more, replays showed the umpire clearly miscalled the final pitch, a sin unforgivable to the fans cheering on the team of the batter. But clearly, most people felt spitting is never justified, even by righteous anger at an umpire.

Spit as a weapon inflicts not a physical injury, but a violation of personal space and hygiene. There is little to compare the feeling of having someone else's bodily fluid tossed at your body.

There are people with disabilities like Danny who sometimes present challenges. They may do things that are unexpected and often unacceptable by most rules of society. Spitting, for instance, falls into that category. But spitting wasn't the only thing Danny did to express his displeasure. He also liked to swear.

"Danny, did you finish your work?"

"Go to hell, asshole!"

Sometimes the swearing and spitting would happen together. The staff who worked with Danny at the workshop he attended called this an "outburst." An ironic term – a weather forecast of a downpour accompanied by high winds of a sort. Most of the people who worked with Danny had worked with him for years. In meeting after meeting, these two behaviors were discussed as problems that Danny clearly needed to learn to control.

"I don't believe anyone will employ Danny as long as he spits and swears," said the psychologist.

Staff agreed. Said the workshop manager, "How could he hold a job if he acts so gross?"

The professionals convinced his family. They told them, "Until Danny learns to control himself in the workshop, he will be unemployable elsewhere."

Yet year after year the professionals found themselves in these same discussions, reviewing their data on how often Danny was spitting or swearing. They tried special programs in which Danny earned or lost points and privileges based on how he behaved. But their main accomplishment was that they managed to barely contain Danny's misbehavior.

Actually, they had accomplished something significant (or, maybe Danny just got tired of doing it, it was hard to tell). He had stopped spitting at people, and was now mainly spitting on the floor. But he still spit pretty regularly. Danny's file summed it all up. On the cover sheet was a label – the first thing new staff would read. It was even highlighted. It said: SPITTER.

Finally, there came a time when staff took a look at what Danny's day was like, and they decided he was pretty bored. A new staff member wondered at a meeting whether Danny was trying to tell them something with his behavior all these years. The staff decided to stop focusing so much attention on Danny's difficulties. Instead, they began to consider Danny's strengths, interests and gifts. They talked to his family and his friends. And then they talked to Danny. Here's what they learned:

- Danny wanted a real job where he could make real money.
- He liked tools and equipment.
- Danny wanted to be around other guys who liked what he liked: cars and sports.
- He wasn't afraid of hard work. He said it would make him strong with "big muscles."

In fact, the staff realized Danny wanted what most people want – a good job that paid reasonably well where he could do what he liked to do, and most importantly, be around other people he liked who weren't necessarily people with disabilities.

But the staff was still uncertain.

"Now that we know this about Danny, what do we do? He still spits and swears here," commented one.

"I know. If he gets a job, he'll only lose it. This might be a waste of time," came the reply.

"Maybe, but I guess we'll never know unless he gets a chance. Besides, if he loses the job, we'll just be back where we started. And maybe Danny will have learned something important."

So, armed with a vague direction, the staff looked for a job for Danny. And as luck would have it, someone landed him an interview at a distribution center for a catalog company, which had an opening for a material handler on their loading dock. It seemed like a busy place. Trucks would come and go. Boxes of goods would have to be loaded, unloaded, shipped, stored, and entered into a database.

To the shock of the staff, Danny did great at the interview. He didn't swear at all. And he spit only once on the floor on the way out, but no one seemed to notice.

So, despite the trepidation of the staff, Danny started his new job. Bob, an employment consultant who had known Danny for years, was assigned to support Danny and his co-workers for a while until Danny learned the ropes. And of course, Bob was to be around in case Danny had one of his "outbursts."

And it wasn't too long before Bob saw Danny spitting. And soon after that he saw Danny swearing. But to Bob's surprise, no one seemed to respond. When Bob returned to work at the end of the week for a staff meeting, everyone asked him how it went.

"Well, you won't believe it," he said.

"Try us. Is he spitting?"

"Uh huh. Spits as much there as he does here."

"How about swearing?"

"If anything, I'd say it's increased."

"Well, I guess we should be prepared for him to get fired and come back here," they said.

"I don't think so."

"Why not? You said he's spitting and swearing, so..."

"Oh, sure he still spits and swears, but there are seven other guys who work there. And you know what? They all spit and swear."

The silence reflected each staff member deep in thought.

"They all swear...and spit?" someone finally ventured.

"Yup. It's sort of the thing on the loading dock. Even the receptionist who comes out every so often, and she's an elderly lady, let's fly a cuss now and then."

Employability Is Not a Magic Line to Cross

Each work culture is unique. Each has its own expectations, norms, and rules. We often assume a certain standard of behavior must exist in all workplaces. Generally that's true. But there are so many exceptions and variations to those standards that it pays to consider a cultural "fit" for many people who may be considered unemployable due to their behavior. What might be a deficit in one setting could well be of no consequence, or even an advantage, in another.

There are people like Danny who challenge us. But the important thing is that those of us who help individuals with disabilities need to consider everyone as employable. Historically, we have made people prove they were employable, by reaching some artificial "magic level" at which they were considered job-ready. Of course, as we have discussed, this often meant years of training in segregated environments practicing work for little or no pay.

I do not believe there is a magic level to get to. Everyone can work.

The problem is how to make this happen for those people who have few experiences or readily identifiable, marketable skills. Also, many people with severe disabilities have had little opportunity to develop their job-seeking skills. For example, I still remember accompanying a young man on his first job interview. When asked if he smoked, he replied, "Only when I am on fire." That was one job offer that didn't come. But he learned from that experience, and eventually he had a good interview and landed a job.

Once a young woman we were working with landed her first job. To our amazement at the time, she received a benefits package that included life insurance. When it was explained to her, she had a terrific response: "Why do they call it a benefit if you have to die to get it?" I still think she had a good point.

I can't say that we have figured employment out for everyone with significant disabilities yet; there are still those who are waiting. But the problem is as much with us, the disability professionals, than it is with any particular skill some might lack. And that is a significant difference. As for the vast majority of people with disabilities who toil in workshops and day treatment programs, we absolutely do know the process of finding them jobs.

I am not arguing that people cannot enhance their employability with training and developing new skills. I think employability is a continuum that offers more opportunities when one has more skills, and also more social connections and experiences. So developing a skill set is a great thing to do. But for most people with disabilities, the place to do that is *on the job*, not in a segregated facility doing unappealing work.

Work Success Depends on Social Belonging

I view community employment as a tool for people with disabilities who have historically been segregated – a tool to help them join the rest of us in life. Employment goes beyond wages, which are so important, and into social belonging. A job is a valued social role, a networking opportunity, and a chance to strut your stuff when the job match is right.

Several years ago, a woman named Sal got her very first job in a medical office. But from her first day on the job, she seemed to be causing her six co-workers difficulties. Sal was misfiling papers, misplacing mail, and, worst of all, committing the cardinal sin in an office, jamming the copy machine.

The fact that Sal was working at all was something of a miracle to Steve, her rehabilitation counselor. He had never believed it possible. Sal had been evaluated several times, and all the tests had come back with the same recommendations: she required more training in a sheltered environment before she would be ready for a workplace. And with her level of mental functioning, her forgetfulness, and her relatively slow speed of production, she was considered "unemployable."

But new funding had been made available, and it was targeted to people who had been labeled as unemployable. Supported employment was designed for people like Sal who likely would need long-term help on a job site.

When the company's office manager, who had a niece with an intellectual disability, heard about the supported employment idea, he whole-heartedly agreed to try it out. His enthusiasm, however, wasn't shared by all the office workers. Six of the eight women who worked there mostly ignored Sal. The other two were polite, but they kept their distance as well.

One day, about three weeks after Sal had started, the women at the office began planning a surprise party for Helen, a long-time co-worker who was retiring from the company. All the ladies where Helen worked were invited. Fortunately, the party would be hosted by one of the women who seemed most open to Sal working there, and Sal soon received an invitation to her first work party.

This presented somewhat of a challenge to the staff who supported Sal at home. She lived in a group home with four other people who had labels of mental retardation. The staff who provided assistance at the home were mystified about how to help Sal prepare for the party, having never had a resident attend something like this outside of the agency. Sal would need to bring a gift, and she would need a nice, new outfit to wear. Sal and Norm, a group home staff member, spent the Friday evening before the event at the mall.

The day of the event arrived and I drove over to pick up Sal and drop her off at the party. As we headed down the road, I looked over at Sal and at the gift she was holding. It was a gift bag.

"So, what did you buy Helen?" I asked nervously.

"Oh, some scented candles."

"Really? That sounds perfect. I am sure she will like them."

What I didn't know was that Sal had spent the night wrapping twelve individual candles, each with its own paper and ribbon. She probably used a whole roll of Scotch tape.

I later heard from one of the women at the party that they couldn't believe she had done this. They were all so touched. Because Sal was so excited, the guest of honor even felt obliged to open each candle. I can only imagine them taking hours to open and wearily pass around every scent.

But the important thing for Sal was that her work situation had changed dramatically. On Friday, she was an outsider who jammed the copy machine and annoyed people. On Monday, she was one of the gang, still jamming the copy machine, but no longer annoying everyone else. Her workmates took her under their wing, showed her the tricks of running the copy machine, and also helped her learn other key rules, like "how to look busy when the boss comes in."

Take Two Verbal Prompts and Call Me in the Morning

We, of course, as disability professionals, could not offer Sal the kinds of tips she needed for job survival in that particular work setting. We simply are not aware of most of them, because we can never be well-versed for every unique workplace culture.

Thus, our job should not necessarily be to dissect a workplace and learn its tasks in order to teach them to the worker with a disability. Our primary task is to help the worker belong so that the other workers who are there day in and day out will offer him or her support and instruction, as well as guidance navigating the cultural norms and expectations there. Sometimes that kind of support is lacking, and the disability professional will need to step in. But in my mind, this is the last resort, not the first thing to do.

Most social behaviors at work can be divided into two areas: those that relate to work, and those that don't. Studies have shown that, depending on the type of work and work setting, most workers spend a good deal of time talking to their co-workers at work.[62, 63] Some of these interactions are required to do a job. But the vast majority of interactions at work are not really required by the employer. They are extra or informal interactions. They include greetings, teasing, joking, sharing personal information, coffee or meal breaks, and giving/seeking advice.

Initially, disability professionals rarely incorporated these interactions when they supported workers with severe disabilities. We viewed them as peripheral to the real work at hand, learning the task of the job itself. But as employment professionals have come to better understand the importance of these interactions, we also have begun to value the need for supporting social acceptance of the worker on the job. Employers generally tend to focus on task-related social skills, and rate non-task interactions as less important for employment success. In actuality, successful workers are those who perform job-related skills and socially interact competently.

Social interactions are the basis for friendships on the job. While employers often do not see the benefit of this, these relationships can be crucial to the functioning of a cohesive work culture. This contributes to an employee's social support. Having an effective support system may mean the difference between being integrated or being isolated within the work environment and culture.

And social isolation is exactly what the problem has been for many workers with disabilities in jobs. While employees with disabilities were just as likely to be involved in job-related interactions as their co-workers, they are less likely to be involved in non-job-related interactions during breaks and work periods.

The issue at first was related to proximity. In the early days of supported employment, many workers with disabilities still were physically segregated from their non-disabled co-workers. Studies have found that employees placed in mobile work crews and enclaves were far less involved with co-workers than individually placed workers. They became socially isolated from their co-workers or had no opportunity for interaction. State Olson and Furgeson, the authors of one such article:

> *"This attitude toward support staff [that they were disability experts], coupled with the enclave model itself, created an island of supported employees and their staff. While these supported employees were not as segregated as sheltered employees, the opportunities for natural supports and relationships seem diminished."* [64]

This fact is one more reason that I no longer consider group placements such as crews and enclaves, besides the issue of their congregation of people based on their disability, as a best practice. Further research has shown that, although the employees with disabilities came in closer proximity to their non-disabled co-workers than they would in a sheltered workshop, they were not involved in the necessary interactions that could lead to the formation of friendships.

Becoming a member of a work culture – achieving a true sense of belonging – is not a simple matter of showing up or expressing an intent to join. The membership of a work culture varies with the expectations of its members on what makes up "belonging." Some cultures have initiation rites, waiting periods, or required participation in activities before a member is considered "one of the gang." Each workplace has its own culture with a wide range of defining characteristics. For instance, there may be an informal dress code, an expectation to take turns buying the coffee, or a work requirement that a specific task always gets done first.

When an employee with a disability first approaches a work setting, he or she is unsure of the rules and expectations and may have difficulty assessing and joining the culture. One role of an individual providing support is to assist the employee in this activity. A preliminary step is to understand the culture of a workplace. Some aspects of culture are not readily apparent and may require becoming a bit of an anthropologist or social detective. Once we begin to understand the norms, rules and expectations, we can support the individual to participate in socially acceptable ways in the workplace.

A wide variety of strategies is available to facilitate what we like to call "inclusion." This is just a fancy way of saying we need to help people fit in so that they belong to the gang that works where they do. Most workers with significant disabilities require a support person to adopt a different role than that of "job trainer." Teaching complex social skills is not something that always can be accomplished with just task analysis and training technology.

My friend and colleague David Mank, a true pioneer in supported employment, puts it nicely:

"...community employment for people with disabilities is an issue of helping people be a part of the fabric of the community, the fabric of the workplace. It is a matter of helping shape connections, personal networks, and opportunities. It is not about having paid professionals providing all of the assistance that every person with a significant disability will ever need." [65]

Self-Employment

With the challenges in job discrimination and the difficulties in finding a good job related to a person's interests, some people with disabilities have begun to explore starting their own businesses. In recent years, there has been great interest in this notion of self-employment for people with disabilities. Small business development opportunities have even been extended to people with more challenging disabilities, including those with particularly high unemployment, such as people with intellectual disabilities, autism, psychiatric disabilities, and severe physical disabilities.

Many disability advocates have welcomed this trend. They note that historically there were many barriers to people with disabilities who wanted to start their own businesses. Studies have identified a lack of supports, discouragement from rehabilitation professionals, and obstacles in planning and financing.

In a 1998 U.S. government report, self-employment options for people with disabilities were cited as often overlooked by employment programs. In 1997, only 2.7% of the 223,668 people who went to a state vocational rehabilitation office and were successfully "closed" became self-employed. This compares to approximately 18% of people nationwide who choose to work for themselves.[66]

But as the movement toward greater self-determination has grown, so has the idea that those people who want to start their own businesses should be given the support to do so. In her book on self-employment, *No More Job Interviews*, Alice Weiss Doyel notes there are several reasons why people with disabilities should consider self-employment. She points out that when you work for yourself, you can choose what you want to do. This might include work you wouldn't normally find through job applications.

Another important advantage is time. Self-employment allows people with disabilities to avoid waiting for acceptance by an employer. By working at home (or at a location of the person's own choosing), transportation, often a challenge or limitation to employment, can become controllable. Within the financial limits of the business, a person with disabilities can create his or her own accommodations, whether related to equipment or flexible work times.

Self-employment offers opportunities to define the job to fit abilities as well as disabilities or the availability of appropriate assistance and support. Owning a business also can allow for the accumulation of assets and help counter the stereotype of dependency and impoverishment faced by individuals with disabilities.[67]

With all these advantages, it would seem like self-employment would be an ideal choice for many people with severe disabilities, particularly in rural or high unemployment areas. And in fact, there has been an increase in people choosing self-employment. The 1998 Rehabilitation Act Amendments made self-employment a priority within the vocational rehabilitation system, and various states have developed projects in small business development.

Out of Workshops and into Real Work

Whether it is finding a job through supported employment or starting your own business, decent individualized employment in the real world is a ticket for a better life for everyone. This is especially true for those with disabilities who are impoverished and not highly valued because they have some difference. To waste this opportunity for so many people with disabilities, especially now that we know how to facilitate it, is unconscionable.

Sheltered workshops and other forms of group employment for people with disabilities should be phased out now. But the reality is that these failing segregated services are actually growing in numbers every day because of their political clout, established funding, and the inertia of the status quo.

While consulting with one disability agency, I ran into another problem in dealing with workshops that has come up often for me since then. This agency ran a sheltered workshop for about sixty-five people. It was making an effort to develop a community employment program as well. As I began to help the job placement staff find work opportunities for individuals who were eager to get started, the workshop director complained to senior management that she was "losing too many of her sheltered workers."

A contemporary typical sheltered workshop. Photo courtesy APSE: The Network on Employment

To me, this is like saying, "I need to keep people with disabilities hostage here in order to meet my production needs." This is a classic example of losing sight of why the agency exists in the first place and what type of thinking the disability industrial complex can breed. Is this agency's mission to meet some workshop production level or to help people lead better lives?

Yet another disability agency told me that while they wanted to expand their community employment program, they also wanted to maintain their workshop. One of the key reasons for doing so was that the workshop could act as a "safety net" for those people with disabilities who lose their jobs.

I can think of no worse situation than using a sheltered workshop as a place to go after someone has managed to leave behind a segregated facility, only then to experience a job loss. For one thing, many workshops do not offer full-time employment. There is frequent "down time," when there is no work available to do. During these periods, people generally sit around, play bingo, go bowling, or watch videos. Hardly the things to do when you need a new job. Job loss should not be arranged to be a devastating event, but it should convey a sense of urgency. Losing my job should not mean I just go back to my old routine and take it easy.

I think we need a better metaphor than offering people a "safety net." I think we should offer a "trampoline." When you lose a job, you need to get right back into the job market. This is also a time to reassess your skills and learn from your accomplishments and mistakes. We should be providing individualized support in resumé building, interview skills, and new work skills. Returning to the workshop to watch videos or work on some production task you probably won't need isn't likely to help. People need an incentive to get back to work.

The few disability agencies that have tried to evolve their segregated employment services to be fully integrated have had little support for their efforts. Only a small number have succeeded in doing away with their work facility and completely converting to a real jobs program. A number of others have managed to "down-size" their segregated operations, eventually reaching a smaller number of people served in their facilities.

Workshops, it turns out, are like hemorrhoids. If you really try, you can shrink them. But they're tough to make go away.

π—0

CHAPTER EIGHT

People Need Homes, Not Residential Facilities

*"In typical residential services...people [with develop-
mental disabilities] have virtually no personal or social
space to call their own, and the ways they are required to
live enforce their social isolation. Efforts to question or
challenge conditions are often defined as
symptoms of inappropriate behavior."*

– John O'Brien

Close to a half a million people with developmental disabilities live in residential placements outside of their fam-
ily-home in the U.S. Of these, over a third live in large group
settings of seven or more people who also have disabilities.[68]
Many of the remaining people also live in group settings, only
smaller in number.

When my job as an executive director in New Hampshire
made me responsible for several group homes, the first thing
I did was to ask to visit them. This immediately created a dilemma. I wanted to be able to see for myself what the reality
was, and visiting unannounced would be the best way to do
that. I certainly had the authority to drop in. And although
the staff initially seemed a bit taken aback by my intention,
they were very ready to accommodate me.

But was this right? Was this authority something I or
my staff deserved? I wondered why I or a group home man-

ager could decide when a guest could come to someone's home, especially with the intention of basically inspecting it. Shouldn't the residents have some control over this?

Sharing a meal at an agency home that supported individuals with disabilities in 1986. I was the executive director of the agency at that time.

The answer is that, in many respects, the kinds of things we take for granted in our own homes do not apply in group homes, where rules often are imposed either for the needs of the landlord or the agency, or for the communal good of the residents and staff as a whole. Instead of making choices based on preferences, the rules dictate how life proceeds based on the lowest common denominator – what is manageable for everyone.

I distinctly remember one group home resident complaining to me that he had to go to the movies one Saturday, and he didn't want to. But most of the residents wanted to go, and it was a planned "community excursion." Since the staff couldn't cover both places, no one could be left behind. While it was great that an effort was being made to help people get into their community, the plans were not individualized, nor were they under the control of each resident. This kind of thing happens all too often, from selecting meals to choosing what is on television.

It also can be expensive to fund a group home. Consider round the clock staffing, the costs of the home, maintenance, food, furnishings, etc. And because there needs to be an accounting for all these expenditures, the funding agent sets up various expectations. These are designed for the safety and well-being of the people who live there. They also create something that is less of a home and more of a program.

Simulated Homes Are Not the Same as Real Homes

Somewhere along the line in our work providing supports to people with disabilities, we have lost sight of one of the core needs of life – to have a home of your own.

Although homelessness is a significant problem among some people with mental illness, most people with significant developmental disabilities do have a place to live. For many, this is with their families. That generally is a good thing, because a family environment is often the most loving and wonderful there is. But even this is not perfect for everyone. Many young adults with disabilities, like most of us, want to leave their parents' nest and live on their own. And for those who do not, their aging parents become more worried about their son's or daughter's future. What will happen when they can no longer provide care? What will happen when they are gone? Where will their son or daughter live?

Unfortunately, for many people with disabilities, the solution to this housing problem historically has been some sort of institutionalization. Options have ranged from nursing homes to "intermediate care facilities" to state-run and private institutions. I have described such institutional life already, and most people agree (although still not all) that this is not a good way to live.

One of the well-intentioned responses to needless institutionalization by the disability industrial complex has been to develop a community-based residential alternative for people with disabilities – the group home. The group home is sort of like a small college dormitory in a neighborhood, without the college. Group homes range in size from housing a few residents to eight or more. The residents share the kitchen, living, and dining areas. Homes are staffed with human service professionals, usually round-the-clock, to assist in daily living tasks. The vast majority of people with developmental disabilities who receive residential services outside of their family home are in such group, provider-owned models.

As an alternative to institutional life, group homes might seem like a God-send. They are smaller in scale, more personalized, and located in real neighborhoods near real stores, banks, and other services. They are "home-like."

But are they true homes? One standard, I think, is to ask what most of us consider to be a true "home." I ask this question in my seminars. The answers are usually predictable. Home is the place where you feel secure. It is your retreat, where you feel loved and comfortable. It is a place you call your own, decorated in your style. It is a place of privacy, where your possessions are protected and safe. It is a place to take pride in, where you can be yourself.

Does a communal group home meet these standards? It is sometimes hard to tell. For many people with disabilities, living in a group home is often the first time they have lived outside the institution or the family. The greater sense of independence people experience is often enough for a resident to say, "I like it here. This is my home." That is often the challenge with evaluating satisfaction with a service, or determining that the person has been given a choice. Generally, the choice is based only on what the person has known, not on what could be.

Are They Neighbors or Facility Residents?

At one time, Dawn and I lived next door to a small group living situation for three adults with developmental disabilities. It was run by an agency different than the one where I worked. Although much smaller in scale than most group homes at the time, there were still apparent differences in this home from the rest of the neighborhood, in addition to the fact that people with significant disabilities lived there. For one thing, there was staff armed with clipboards coming in and out at all hours of the day and night.

One warm summer evening, I overheard a staff meeting that was occurring on the porch. "Did John have a bowel movement today?" asked one residential staff member. Needless to say, this was not something that needed to be broadcast to the neighborhood.

Dawn and I got to know most of the neighbors in our neighborhood quite well, and we enjoyed socializing with them. But the residents of the group home never managed to do the same, despite some efforts on our part to bring them into this small community's life. For one thing, the staff just weren't interested in socially connecting with neighbors – they were busy with the daily living needs of the residents. And the neighbors' perception of the home was that it was some sort of half-way house for people with undetermined problems. One neighbor even confided his concerns to me, upon hearing from a group home staff member that one of the residents was "non-ambulatory." This term simply means the individual is unable to walk unassisted. But the neighbor said, "I don't want anyone living near me who can't ride in an ambulance!"

The whole situation was a shame. The home stood as an island in the neighborhood, and the residents were marooned there.

Not all group homes are the same, but most of the ones I have visited are run with a nursing-home-like efficiency. Whether due to policies imposed by the funding agent or the agency itself, or due to the staff director who controls things, there are schedules, rules, posted policies, exit signs, and other trappings of facilities. I have even seen some homes with "staff only" rooms.

Recently, I saw this type of mentality while visiting my mother-in-law, who was convalescing in a nursing facility. While Dawn and I were talking with her and discussing a rather serious topic, an aide barged in without knocking, interrupting us. She then proceeded to turn on the television set in the room, tuning it to the local news station. "Got to hear the news," she said, and then busily set about straightening the room, as though we weren't there. It seemed to me we were just other items of furniture to her. There is much to do to take care of patients, and in a medical emergency, an intrusion is to be expected. But there still should be some routine respect for people's personal space. For my mother-in-law, this was her "home" for the time being. But you really couldn't tell that from the way her space was routinely violated.

This type of interaction happens because there is a group treatment effect that develops in group homes, nursing homes, and institutions. One might be more home-like and attractive than another, but they all share a sense of purpose that is less about home, and more about people management. I have visited numerous group homes with lighted "exit" signs, and I have seen kitchens with menus posted for the next month. I don't think this is how most of us live. What if we don't want ham tonight? The answer in a congregate setting is "too bad."

Once again, my point is not that all group homes are bad places, run by evil people intent on controlling the lives of others. It is the group residential model that is dysfunctional. It leads to compromises most of us wouldn't even consider. Even well-run, benevolent agencies can find themselves setting policies and procedures that impose rules people shouldn't have to deal with in their own homes. And the grouping issues I discussed earlier (people with disabilities living together maximizing the stigma they experience) still play a part in how neighbors perceive the people who live in group homes.

Group living makes it convenient for others to perceive all the residents as a collective, and this type of thinking leads to stereotyping. Labeling the living arrangement only strengthens this thinking. When we consider a "military base," or a "college dorm," we can envision the typical people living there. Unfortunately, the same is true of a "ghetto."

Supported Living

Like supported employment, supported living grew out of the early eighties and was designed to focus on people individually. In this model, residential supports are based on the individual strengths, preferences, and needs of people with disabilities in their preferred communities – the places they want to live. Supported living is based on the principle of self-determination. This maintains that people have a right to live in their own homes, stay connected to families and communities of origin, and choose what they want to do, with whom, when, and how they want to do it. It presumes that people need more than just a place to live where they will receive training and someone to provide assistance to them.

This approach has proven to be highly promising, although just a relatively small number of people live this way when compared to the group facility model of housing. There are several recognized essential elements of supported living. But the main one is that people will have homes of their own that they control. This includes selecting homes within their means, as well as choosing whom they will live with or receive supports from. This is far different than being referred to an open slot in some residential facility or group home.

Because there is no one right way to set up a supported living model, people using supported living services are in all kinds of homes and neighborhoods. Some live with a paid roommate, some have staff that come in and help them out, and others have some other kind of arrangement. They live in apartments by themselves or with friends or roommates, or in houses or condominiums, in rural, urban, and suburban areas. But their names are on the lease or deed. There is no mistaking whose home it is.

The support isn't fixed, either. It is flexible and depends on what people need. Some people might require intensive assistance for personal care, while others just need help with budgeting or cooking. There is a lot of creativity. Sometimes the support comes from family, neighbors, and friends, as well as from paid professionals. But when there is a paid professional, the relationship is different than with the traditional human service agency. It is the person with a disability who has hired his or her help, perhaps with the support of others. The person with a disability will have interviewed and negotiated duties and wages. This means the staff, as in any other client-professional relationship, must meet the expectations of their employer, or they could be terminated.

Supported living isn't a free ride. There are budget restraints, like in the real world. The more an individual earns or has access to, the more choices he or she has about a home and lifestyle.

In supported living, people have more to say about defining the lifestyles they want, instead of living according to regulations. In order to ensure this, the selection and financing of housing is kept separate from the selection and financing of disability services and supports. In other words, the landlord should not be the same entity as the giver of support. In that case, there would be too much control over the individual by one party.

This is hard to accept by many disability agencies. They control supports and often own the group homes. They thus have a vested interest in keeping people in agency-owned homes.

Group Home Compromises

In 2000, I was a project evaluator for an agency that had a state grant to develop individualized affordable housing for people with disabilities. The agency was well-run, staffed by caring people, and really wanted to help people with disabilities find good housing. They had run group homes, and were now moving into supported living. In the process of my review, it became clear to me that the housing and support functions could not be controlled by the same agency without compromising the self-determination of those who lived in their homes.

For example, in one home, residents disagreed over the desired temperature in the home. Each person would change the thermostat to such an extent that it was either very cold or very warm, causing everyone distress. After much discussion by house staff, it was decided to set the temperature at a "comfortable level" and install a thermostat lock. Now I know some households where this kind of battle goes on between husband and wife, yet they haven't resorted to an outsider coming in and "locking down" the thermostat.

I felt this was an inappropriate solution that infringed on the rights of individuals to have access to their thermostat, and I suggested some alternative approaches to the agency. But this example illustrates the inherent dangers when a provider also controls a person's property. It permits too much influence over how an individual or set of roommates lives. Although the agency proceeded with deliberation, there was still a need for outside advice to change a landlord/provider decision.

Ultimately, the project succeeded in many ways in providing attractive and affordable homes for people with disabilities, although there remained issues of group size and control. The residential agency finally split into two agencies, one for housing and one for supports. This was a difficult process, and not one most agencies would choose to follow. But it illustrates the kind of deconstruction necessary for the DIC to reinvent itself.

In another instance, an agency developed the following criteria a resident must comply with in order to live in their housing program: "The individual must be willing to co-operate regarding showing of the homes to individuals or groups interested in the program."

Notice how the word "program" is used interchangeably with "home." How would you like that little phrase, "...must be willing to cooperate..." when we want to tour your home, in your mortgage, lease, or condo association agreement? Such a policy needs to greater reflect the rights of residents to privacy. There should be an option to negotiate visitation, allowing for the need, with appropriate notice, for the landlord to occasionally visit properties at reasonable times and with reasonable frequency.

Because all householders have the same right to privacy, any home visit should require agreement of the individuals ahead of time. It should be conducted with sensitivity, courtesy, respect, and restraint from unwarranted intrusion. Except for life-threatening emergencies, an individual's home should be entered only when the individual extends an invitation or permission. After my intervention, the agency subsequently, if not a bit reluctantly, changed the policy.

Generally, in my experience, most agencies "allow" a good deal of residential control over the decorations of the home. However, this is done at their benevolence and not by design. And even with a benevolent landlord, issues still arise. For example, two years ago, one agency decided to place a permanent sign on a house to reflect fundraising or donations from a local civic group.

Again, I questioned the wisdom of displaying public civic fundraising support for a private residence, as it would add a stigma of charity to the people with disabilities who lived there. Agency management replied it was a necessary part of fundraising and any signs would be small and "tastefully" designed. I further disagreed, stating the presence of such signs of any size would be inappropriate, and that there are other avenues to express thanks and provide public recognition to fundraising bodies. Ultimately, the agency decided to put up the signs anyway. Fundraising was too important. And these are rather minor issues compared to what can happen in agencies where there is less review and open discussion.

Affordable Housing

Supported living has provided more individualized and normalized living options for citizens with developmental disabilities than any other residential approach. But one of the barriers to supported living is the lack of affordable housing. This difficulty has been problematic throughout the U.S.

According to *Priced Out in 2000*, a report published by the Consortium for Citizens with Disabilities, in 2000, there was not one single housing market in which people receiving Supplemental Security Income (SSI), a Social Security benefits program, could afford to rent an efficiency or one-bedroom apartment. On average, people with disabilities receiving SSI needed to pay nearly 98% of their SSI checks in order to rent a modest one-bedroom unit at the published HUD Fair Market Rent. And the cost of living adjustments to SSI benefit levels have not kept pace with the cost of rental housing. Between 1998-2000, rental-housing costs rose almost twice as much as the income of people with disabilities.[69]

To make the goal of individualized community living a reality for people with disabilities, more affordable housing options are needed in communities across America. Increased housing production not only will increase the availability of affordable housing, it will dramatically increase the number of rental units that are accessible to people with disabilities as required by the Fair Housing Amendments Act of 1988.

In a review of housing for people with disabilities, the National Council on Disability stated:

> *"Shortages of affordable housing are widely recognized as representing one of the major problems facing people of moderate and low incomes in our country today. For people with disabilities, this problem is even more acute, because affordability is also conditioned by inaccessibility, availability, and discrimination. According to a recent study, while levels of home ownership for most Americans are at near historic highs, rates of home ownership for Americans with disabilities remain shockingly low, languishing in the single digits."* [70]

Most individuals with developmental disabilities cannot afford market rents in many areas, leaving them with limited housing options. They are then faced with renting apartments in undesirable areas, sharing their homes with others in similar circumstances, or moving into facilities and group homes that congregate people based on their deficits.

Home Ownership

Part of the American Dream has always been home ownership. This is yet another aspect of life denied to most people with significant disabilities. When one considers the huge public expenditures over the years on housing people with disabilities, including property acquisition, upkeep, and taxes, there is hardly any accumulated personal equity for the individuals themselves. There is, however, growing equity by the non-profit and for-profit agencies that provide services and the housing itself.

In the early nineties, the Institute on Disability at the University of New Hampshire ran a three-year project to promote home ownership for people with disabilities. Nineteen people who participated in the project became homeowners. Only half of the these people were employed at the time. Their labels included mental retardation, cerebral palsy, autism, and psychiatric disabilities. Three quarters were further labeled as having "severe" or "profound" disabilities. Probably there were two main things that were learned. One, disability labels should not stop anyone from home ownership. Two, funding from the disability service system, if used creatively, can support people down the path to a mortgage and owning their homes. [71]

There are now ongoing projects throughout the U.S. that provide individuals and those helping them with support to overcome the numerous financial and societal barriers to home ownership for people with disabilities. One such barrier, for example, is that people with disabilities are usually recipients of public benefits. Such benefits have resource restrictions, which prohibits them from saving money for a down payment on a mortgage. But a mix of private and public funds, including grants and low or no interest loans, can solve this barrier.

Solving the housing needs of individuals who are vulnerable in our society, including those with significant disabilities, can be challenging. But there is a vision that holds much promise. Housing, self-owned or not, should be individualized and based on people's preferences, work decisions, and resources. There are creative ways to finance affordable housing, and imaginative ways to finance home ownership. When we do this, we open the doors to community membership. After all, there really is "no place like home." And, I might add, there is also "no other place quite like a group home."

CHAPTER NINE

Supporting Self-Determined Lives: One Person at a Time

*"If you could only know me for who I am
Instead of for who I am not,
There would be so much more to see
'Cause there's so much more than I've got.
So long as you see me as mentally retarded,
Which supposedly means something I guess,
There is nothing that you or I could ever do
To make me a human success."*

– Marc Gold

Some people define success with money, power, or fame. But I think richness comes from two main things: first, the people in your life; and second, how close you are to living your life the way you dream it should be.

And if I had to categorize the two main issues that challenge people with disabilities again and again, I would say that it would be isolation and powerlessness. They often have few people with authentic connections to them in their life and little control over how they can live.

Many of the people with disabilities I have worked with in my career had to deal with a profound sense of loneliness based on impoverishment, both of money and experiences, and isolation. Without experiences in life or the resources to do things, what do we really know about ourselves, and how do we connect to others?

When you add up all the discrimination, labeling, grouping, and segregating, plus the challenge of the disability itself, for most people having a good life still boils down to the variety and quality of relationships they can experience. And for people with severe disabilities, their relationships are often dominated by professional staff, people paid to be with them, a disturbing realization that must impact one's self esteem. Those who are lucky also have their family and a few other people with similar disabilities in their lives, some of whom are friends, and some of whom are simply assigned to be in their home as housemates or in their daytime program.

A quality life also involves the amount of control people have in choosing among life's paths to reach their own hoped-for destiny. Self-determination is the term most often used to describe the process of people with disabilities self-directing their own life goals and behavior. This concept should also be the basis for changing the service system we have. For people with disabilities, the challenge has been to balance promoting autonomy with providing safe and secure settings. Thus far, the mistake disabilities services have made is to err on the side of over-sheltering people.

People Call the Shots in Their Lives

The person being served, with the support of family and significant others, must decide the supports they need based on their preferences and life goals. Self-determination is a core element of basic human rights. And when, because of a disability, an individual is judged to not be competent to make life decisions, then it is up to the guardian to make the best guess of what the person with a disability would want.

This must be based on informed choice and a trusting relationship. There is a lot of lip service given to this idea, but too often it is not the reality.

Also, real self-determination regarding the service system would include control over how money is spent on one's services. There are efforts going on now to test this notion on a small scale. (Only about half of the states report offering "consumer-directed" funding.)[72] I have advocated for some time that funding entities need to measure outcomes and customer satisfaction, in addition to what they primarily do now, which is completing quality checklists and conducting file reviews of agencies' policies and procedures. These results should be aggregated and posted on the web and in other accessible media. We should then create a sort of rating system like Morningstar does with mutual funds, awarding one to five stars based on a set of quality standards.

Say, for example, Mike was a person with a disability who wanted assistance with employment where he lived. He and his advocates could compare each of the disability or generic employment agencies that provide such assistance in his area, noting how many people were employed, how long it took to find a job, what kind of starting wages people had, etc. Mike would probably seek out a five-star employment agency, and the one- and two-star programs would soon need to clean up their acts or fall by the wayside. That is the difference between a market economy and a overly socialized one.

If we were to give individuals control over how their funding gets spent, and also provide them with good information about which agencies perform well on whatever is most important to them, then I think market forces would begin to influence the system in positive ways.

Flexible Supports, One Person at a Time

Whenever I hear the word "model," as in our "autism program model," or "day treatment model," I flinch. This means we will try to fit people to what professionals do, rather than supporting them in what they want to do. There is nothing wrong with using a flexible approach based on a model, such as supported employment or supported living or positive behavior supports. But these types of models must continually reinvent themselves, and must offer as many ways of providing specific support as there are people.

As soon as we try to come up with a housing, employment, or training solution prescribed to a disability or imbedded in some fixed model, we lose individuality. For many programs, the most convenient method of service delivery is to provide a "package" of pre-designed services. While this sometimes can produce desired results all in one setting, many times people receive greater benefit from a constellation of services. And the services may come from a variety of settings, including agencies, private business, individuals, or others from the community.

Contrast that to how planning is usually done now. People with disabilities are referred to fixed choices of programs – they can go to agency A or B or have no options at all. It is reminiscent of Henry Ford offering his Model T in "any color so long as it's black." Since programs have pre-established entrance and exit criteria, much of their efforts go into making people fit their scheme of things. This is known as a Hobson's Choice. It dates back to the seventeenth century England, where Thomas Hobson ran a livery stable. He rented his horses in a strict order. If a customer came in and asked if he could choose a horse, Hobson would answer "Of course, as long as you take the one nearest the door."

Instead of offering a Hobson's Choice (whatever program openings, known as "slots," that an agency currently has), the service system needs to facilitate and coordinate an array of supports. They should be negotiated with whatever and whomever are available in the community, so that the person can approach the quality of life he or she wishes.

People with disabilities generally have received services and life supports with other people who share their disability label. Since most services have tended to be segregated, this has left people limited and isolated in their education, living, work, and recreation. It also generally provided few role models or peer trainers, nor a diversity of relationships. Services should be individualized, and flexible supports built around each person where they wish to live, work, and socialize, so that people experience the rich fabric of community life.

Disability professionals should research and provide as many alternatives as possible for achieving what a person with a disability wants to happen. For a position such as a "case coordinator," this means looking into possibilities far beyond what looks at first glance to be the most likely alternative. For instance, if someone says I want a new place to live, that should not translate to a placement in a group home, simply because a local agency has an opening. Options must be fully explored, so there can be a better understanding of what is available, what might have been missed, or what needs to be created.

Beneficial Relationships Based on Commonality

If we have good relationships, we have friendship, companionship, meaning, and support when we need it. My wife and I count ourselves lucky because, in addition to our families, we have a strong network of social connections in the community where we live. For the last five years, we have been part of a social circle that revolves around "Casserole Night." Seven families, all with children, get together every other week for a pot-luck dinner. The host family rotates among each of us. It is a lot of good food and conversations, running jokes, and warm camaraderie. Our children have become fast friends, and we have taken group excursions together, such as camping trips and weekend getaways.

We love them all dearly, and being a part of this group enriches our lives. These are not our only friends, and the other families who are part of Casserole Night also have other social circles they belong to. But the strong social capital from having these ties and from our other close friends becomes evident in times of need. When one of us is sick, there is dinner delivered to our door, offers of childcare, or someone calling and volunteering to drive our daughter to school. Most importantly, there is emotional support. We know there are people who care about what happens to us. And of course we in turn care about their lives, and reciprocate as events occur. It is a given in life that things will occur that will upset our comfort and routines, so having this kind of assistance and caring is invaluable.

Most of the successes professionals have had helping individuals with disabilities have come when we or they have fostered such strong social connections. Those relationships take people into places that disability professionals cannot go. In the sociological literature, this phenomenon has been termed "social capital." It refers to what I have described – how our ties to people allow us to call on them to do things for us, with the expectation of reciprocity. This feature of support can range from small favors (Will you give me a ride?) to life-saving (You can live with me for a while.) Social capital can be incredibly important in the lives of people with disabilities.

Not that non-disabled people in our current society are doing such a great job with fostering strong social ties. In the book *Bowling Alone*, Robert Putnam notes a disturbing social disengagement in society. He uses the example of how between 1980 and 1993, the total number of bowlers in America increased by 10%, while league bowling decreased by 40%. This rise of solo bowling itself is not so important, but it is symptomatic of a greater loss, that of the conversations over beer and pizza that league bowlers enjoy.[73]

The internet and technology also have managed to reduce daily interpersonal connections everywhere. We pick up "take-out" for our food, shop over the web, and chat via social web sites such as MySpace.com. We e-mail and text message constantly. And in the places where people used to converse, such as waiting in a line, people are already in conversation on their cell phones. We even can check ourselves out at the store without a cashier. Our custom of sharing touchstones from television, hit songs, movies, and the like are gradually disappearing as people use technology to pursue their own interests.

Geography and physical proximity are slowly declining as the defining factors in social culture as we connect in other ways through interactions that are not person-to-person. These technological connections are generally weak ties. While this trend offers us all the opportunity to be more efficient, or to pursue very individualistic interests, we lose something important.

Humans are social beings. Our memories of life are filled not with text messages, but with shared events with other people in our lives. Our social networks provide support, mental health, and a sense of belonging.

People with disabilities need to be a part of that, too. Our services must first of all not segregate them from the places where people live, work, and play in their communities. Our services also must not create "differentness" by being too artificial, jargon-filled, and centered on labels and groupings of people with like disabilities. Instead, we need to help them learn how to apply the social glue needed for relationships to form.

Eligibility Is about Deficits; Support Is about Capacity

To get help and access any disability service system, people with disabilities must first prove themselves as having sufficient deficits to qualify. This is no small task. Since the confirming of disability for funding requires a search for deficits, this mindset has in turn produced a deficit remediation service plan – a type of "fix what's wrong" approach. The resulting file of information not only gets people in the funding door, but from then on labels them and prescribes their future.

But our life successes flow from our capacities and talents, not our deficits. Working on our shortcomings is fine, but not to the point that it defines our whole life. It is much better to "follow your bliss...and doors will open where you didn't know they were going to be," as mythology expert Joseph Campbell[74] has said, even if it appears unrealistic on the surface. On the path to achieving life goals and dreams, we will all need accommodation, training, support, and creative workarounds for the problems encountered. That is where the disability system should offer assistance.

A better way of thinking is to help people pursue meaningful lives by exploring their dreams, hopes, interests and capabilities. We should focus on each person's positive attributes as the starting point for offering assistance. Once their life direction and the attributes they will bring to the table are better understood, then supports and services can be created. Some of these will build on strengths, while others will negotiate needs. But all services revolve around each person's wishes, and not some arbitrary fix-it list.

A meaningful job and home in the community should be an option for everyone, regardless of label or perceived deficits. This idea is in direct contradiction to traditional services, which center on the idea of "feasibility." Feasibility implies that some people are or could be "ready" for a job or a home, while others are not now and perhaps never can be employable or able to live in the community due to the nature of their disabilities. Most persons with significant disabilities in the current rehabilitation paradigm still are considered "not ready for work" and in need of vocational training to overcome a list of deficits.

What makes supported employment and supported living different is that there is a presumption of employability and community readiness for everyone in some place that is related to their interests and skills. What remains is to figure out how to find the right place, along with the types and level of support needed to ensure the success that leads to a satisfying career and home life.

Natural Environments

Right now, the default setting of disability services is set on artificially created programs in segregated facilities, supposedly in the "least restrictive environment." People with disabilities should be able to get assistance or learn new skills while living in their homes, or working in their jobs, or going to their banks, stores, or theatres. We must not make the mistake of thinking we can simulate these places. I have observed far too many simulated grocery stores with empty cereal boxes, and simulated work environments with bags of nuts and bolts, and simulated kitchens with stoves that work nothing like the stoves that people will live with. Using sheltered environments to create an artificial learning setting for people to learn work skills just hasn't worked. Rarely do the time and energy involved have a meaningful, cost-effective link to a real job in business.

Most services for persons with disabilities are still intrinsically linked to the facilities used to deliver those services. Housing special programs for groups of people who share a label tends to highlight the differences of people and says to the community, "This is where these kinds of people should be – away from everyone else." Services and supports need to be offered where life takes place – in workplaces, neighborhoods, stores, and schools where everyone else in the community goes.

Effective Supports That Fit the Setting

We need to provide supports in ways that are both effective and as naturally acceptable as possible to the setting and culture. When we help people in natural environments, we must take care not to add to their stigma of being different because of their disability. Our services should have "natural validity." They should not stand out as artificial, unusual, or obtrusive.

A task analysis-shaping-fading approach, as part of "systematic training," is one of the most effective learning strategies that exists, particularly for people who need extra support with learning. Unfortunately, by reducing all learning to such a precise, clinical level, we have left behind individual differences in style and cultural differences that affect the way things are normally taught from place to place. Teaching should be a partnership, among the learner, the trainer, and the expectations of the setting; the technology is only a tool and it needs to be negotiated among all three.

Another outcome of systematic training procedures has been an over-reliance on disability professionals for all training and support. Since one-on-one training is not a fiscal reality for most services, this has produced more "cost-effective" group training, which comes at a heavy price for all. It has also given out messages of "professionals know best," hindering natural relationships and interactions at work. Studies such as the Harris poll still report high levels of anxiety from the public in relating to people with disabilities. This could be explained in part by the highly clinical and segmented approaches used in human services. For example, people with disabilities have music therapy, art therapy, horticultural therapy, pet therapy and so on, while most other people just plant a garden or own a cat. This specialization of life into slices of therapy does not reflect the totality of life.

Where we work relates to where and how we live. This in turn is connected to our hobbies and interests, which influence how we communicate, which impacts our relationships with our friends and family and on and on.

Professional specialists need to bring their skills to bear within the context of a person's whole life, and not within segmented exercises or activities. Anyone can learn to be a decent trainer or provide personal support to someone with a disability. Indeed, the growth of these diverse relationships opens up new doors to community life for people with disabilities.

Social Roles Valued by the Community

We need to pay much more attention to how well people with disabilities take on the expectations of our culture to work, pay taxes, be a good citizen and neighbor, and reciprocate something back to the community. When people with disabilities are seen as co-workers, neighbors, customers, musicians, photographer, and the like, their identities as individuals with a disabilities are replaced by their more valued social identities.

I remember how Carl, a young man labeled with Down Syndrome I knew, got involved with sponsoring a foster child from El Salvador. He would help with bake sales and other small fund-raising events in order to send some money each month to the young boy, who would write back telling of his life. Carl would have someone read him each letter, then he would share what he learned with those around him. He was very proud of his ability to really help someone in a significant way. This role not only changed his self-perception, it changed how others perceived him as well.

No Disability Labels and Jargon

I recall the time I was in a department store to observe a middle-aged man with a disability, Howard, who worked there. While I watched him folding jeans, a customer came by and rifled through the merchandise he had so carefully folded. He immediately began to stamp his feet and yell, "No, no, no." Needless to say, the customer moved away, and the cashier in charge of the department came running over, along with Suzanne, Howard's staff person from a disability agency who was there to help train him.

Suzanne managed to calm Howard, and she sent him to the breakroom. The cashier immediately looked to Suzanne for an explanation, saying "What's wrong with him?"

Suzanne's response was, "He had a perseverative behavioral outburst. Don't worry, we have a program for it."

The cashier just shook her head and went back to her station. I could only imagine what she was thinking: "What in the heck is a perseverative behavioral outburst? It sounds like a cross between a weather forecast and a psychiatric illness. Whatever it is, it can't be good." Using disability terminology no one understands and specialized programs no one else experiences intimidates others and builds walls that isolate people. When the things non-disabled people work on are disturbed, most of us get *frustrated*. Or we may get *upset, angry,* or even *pissed off.* But according to disability professionals, people like Howard have *perseverative behavioral outbursts.*

Not only did the language mark Howard as being different, but Suzanne's follow-up comment, "we have a program for it," does as well. Howard needs to learn that his job exists because customers will mess up the clothes. He needs to understand that when he is upset, he must not yell in the store. That kind of behavior can lead to losing his job. To help him, Suzanne will first need to have Howard's respect and trust. But Suzanne also must learn that she must not exaggerate his behavior with a label that will make it that much harder to understand.

We need to purge our tendency to speak in labels and terms that no one outside the field knows or understands. I have watched too many non-disabled people in the community be scared off by professionals who explain the behavior of people with disability as perseverative or non-compliant. Others might reference programs or training approaches that are not normally encountered outside the disability field. Still others talk about a goal from an individual service plan (ISP) or some other mandated plan (IHP, IEP, IWRP, etc.). These initials are not easy to comprehend.

Sometimes people with disabilities need specialized accommodations, such as a learning program. But when these are used, whether it is a piece of technology, a service dog,

or some training approach, we need to work to make its use
an acceptable part of everyday life by talking about it in plain
language.

Behavior Change Based on Communication and Trust

We should try to learn what people's behavior means, and
then build a trusting relationship before helping them make
the changes they might need. When someone displays behavior that doesn't fit some arbitrary norm, the most common
reaction I have experienced has been for someone to conduct
an overly simplistic behavior analysis and then institute a behavior program to control, reduce, or modify the behavior.
Environments are then manipulated, reinforcers are controlled, and consequences delivered. Often these programs
are developed without any analysis at all.

Behavior is a form of communication. We first need to
listen closely and explore what an action might represent,
even when it challenges us and others. There is also a context to behavior – its acceptability depends on circumstances,
time, and place. By focusing on the context and communicative intent of what people do, we can build on their strengths
and work with them in partnership, rather than in a power
struggle.

Natural Supports

Nearly every mission statement of agencies that help people with disabilities talks about making people "as independent as possible." While not having to rely on others for most
life needs is important to many of us, the reality is we are all
interdependent on each other in most domains of life to different degrees. My friend and colleague Al Condeluci, in his
book *Interdependence: The Route to Community*, talks about
interdependence as being about mutual acceptance that re-

spects the differences all people have.[75] For too many people with disabilities, independence has translated to loneliness.

Having the skills for self-preservation and care must be balanced with the social networks of support that should be developed and nurtured for each of us. The disability system too often has tried to be a source of social support for people, and this has largely failed. Staff come and go, but the people they serve remain. Our role is not to be the caretaker of first resort, but the caretaker of last resort.

We should instead focus on acting as a facilitator of social, physical, and emotional support from those that are in each person's life. We all need support systems to make our lives sustainable. We need to help people with disabilities build natural support systems instead of artificial ones whenever possible.

Modeling Values

Anyone who is in the field of helping people with disabilities must always model and teach the value that people with disabilities are productive, can learn, and can contribute to a community.

Why are values so important? The answer is that values and attitudes have a large influence on how disability services operate, and even more on how society responds to people with disabilities in their midst. For example, suppose an individual with a severe disability wants a job, and staff disagree over how "ready" the person is, or whether anyone with such a disability can succeed in a community job. These opinions generally have more to do with values than with any rational assessment of the situation, despite our claims of objectivity. We know this because there are so many people currently with jobs through supported employment who professionals, in their best objective judgment, claimed could not work.

One source of values confusion stems from the fact that most professionals are working within multi-service or education agencies. Most of these operate a variety of employment training programs, including segregated day activity, pre-vocational training, work activity or sheltered work models. This situation can put stress on the staff because an array of more traditional services can be in conflict with the values and strategies of non-segregation.

We need to work hard so that others fully expect people with disabilities to have a job, have a home, and be a part of their communities.

Helping People Express Themselves

Taking the time to listen. This is a very simple thing, but it doesn't happen enough. I have been in too many meetings in which professionals sit down and proceed to tell people with disabilities and their families what needs to happen in their lives. This occurs without any significant effort to understand each individual's personal goals, needs, and resources available. It seems to especially happen to individuals who are not very verbal.

Some people have unique ways of expressing their preferences or dislikes. This is particularly true for persons who have difficulty communicating through speech. Often how one acts is the best indicator of personal preferences, feelings, or frustrations. Disability professionals need to learn to try to interpret the reactions and behavior of people with disabilities as they respond to new environments and activities.

We also need to learn from the interpretations of those who know the person best. If Tara flaps her hands, is she anxious, unhappy, or excited? Without knowing the answer, we might not know what Tara is feeling about where she is and what she is doing. But Tara's family, her friends, and others who have shared her life do know more about her emotions based on her behavior. To help Tara, we need their knowledge.

Before taking any action, we should learn about the wishes, desires, and experiences of the person in question. Exploring comments, interpretive gestures, and reactions to situations and people can help everyone become more educated about a person's desires and directions. Listening isn't just limited to an initial meeting. As a service concept evolves, the individual needs to continually evaluate options, make informed decisions, and provide ongoing feedback.

Educated Choicemaking

Helping people make choices requires a commitment to helping them make *informed* choices. For example, it is not uncommon for individuals to express fear about the realities of leaving an institution or acquiring a community job. But this response may be a result of how the opportunity is presented and whether the offer makes sense for the person. Some concerns are based on wanting to wait for the right opportunity, rather than taking just any offering.

The choices people make about work and home should be based on being as fully educated about the options as possible. It is sometimes difficult to try something new when the "new" is so unknown, especially for persons previously considered "unemployable" or "not ready for community life." One possibility is to help people experience the community through volunteer or job shadowing situations. We also can help people to visit friends and acquaintances in various types of homes, so they can see first-hand how people live outside of an institution, facility, or group home. This could provide important information as an individual makes career and residential decisions. It also may make sense for some people to have "no-obligation" tryouts, or a type of situational assessment experience, before they can adequately express a decision about a home or a job.

Flexible Funding

Personal determination and choicemaking can be severely restricted when service options are limited to existing programs. One response to this situation is for the disability service system to provide more flexible funding arrangements for needed services and supports, including more creative options like micro-enterprise developments, cooperative housing, and other innovations.

Respect for the Family

Families who have a family member with a disability face many challenges. They are usually the ones who will always be there to support their family member, as disability programs and staff come and go. Too often their role is dismissed or minimized by disability professionals.

For many years, parents of children with disabilities were given the impression by disability professionals that their children would never be able to do things in the "real world" on their own. The best they might expect for their son or daughter was to be able to live and work in a "protected" environment, where they would be sheltered from the demands of life.

One reason the sheltered workshop and group home system was developed was for families to have an alternative to institutionalization – a safe place for individuals with disabilities to go to have something meaningful to do. For many families, this is no small thing.

Parents have watched disability professionals pass judgments on their family member throughout his or her lifetime. Many times these opinions are conflicting and confusing, and they include multiple labels, diagnoses and placements. No wonder the idea of a community job or a real home is not always warmly embraced by families. It must seem like one more program in a long line of promises.

But the idea of supporting an integrated life in the community holds more than just promises. In its true sense, it represents a break from a past of treating a person's deficits. I have watched people develop in well-matched jobs in ways no one could predict. A real job can affect all aspects of a person's life – in friendships, in self esteem and as a respected contributor and consumer in the community.

And when a person finds a place to really call home, the growth and changes in that individual can infuse an entire family with new energy and possibilities. Other doors become open to consideration, including new living arrangements, recreation and leisure, and an expanding circle of relationships.

Many families will need time and assistance to consider the opportunities and perceived risks in helping their family member to leave the perceived safety of a facility for people with disabilities. The disability system's role is to help provide information and support so families can make educated decisions right from the start.

Questioning Assumptions Respectfully

There is an old proverb I like that says: "He who slings mud loses ground." I have always tried to challenge people in a respectful way when I believed they were preventing someone from realizing the kind of life they wanted and could achieve.

But it is also important not to let people get caught up in previous thinking about a person based on old, untrue, or limited information. "He can't do that; she isn't able to; he isn't ready yet; he refuses to." These statements all need to be examined closely.

Some assumptions can create what is known as a "self-fulfilling prophecy." The mere belief that some people are unable to benefit from an experience can limit their opportunities and expectations. For example, a residential staff person plans to take each resident with whom he works to a local food store to help teach skills related to grocery shopping. Going down the list, he sees Tom's name. He wonders, "Why bother taking Tom to the grocery store? He is not really aware of what we are doing anyway and could never learn to handle money."

And so Tom never gets a chance to experience a new environment, not because he cannot learn something from it, but because someone assumed he couldn't. When others believe you are incapable such that you will not realize a learning possibility, your performance never gets to change – not because it can't, but because no one is supporting you to try. And if you never are given opportunities to learn, your abilities are not likely to improve, and this only reinforces the original assumption. ("See, I told you Tom couldn't count change.")

Checking Satisfaction

One of the most disempowering experiences for people with disabilities is to be considered "successfully served" and forgotten once they have been referred to an agency or placed in a job or home. Careers and residential choices evolve as we grow and change, particularly for people just entering the community. Services don't drop off a cliff; they are ongoing for people with significant disabilities.

The disability system should include a process for continually exchanging feedback and information on the individual's satisfaction with services, the outcomes, and any other issues that relate to their decisions about their career life.

Acceptance of Change

The rapid development and funding growth of disability services over the years has created a huge disability industrial complex, an infrastructure of segregated facilities, regulations, and disability grouping. Agency directors within this system believe they must have people with disabilities attend their programs in their facilities in order to keep their budgets and pay staff salaries, including their own. The tendency to keep things the same and resist change is overwhelming.

But in human services, new ideas, service strategies, and approaches are part of everyday life. The manager who stubbornly sticks to one way of business while the field evolves tells staff it is okay not to be innovative. An open response to suggested change creates an atmosphere of learning and creativity. Walt Whitman gave sage advice when he wrote:

> *"Reexamine all you have been told, At school at church or in any book, Dismiss whatever insults your own soul, And your very flesh shall be a great poem."* [76]

On the other hand, being open to innovation shouldn't translate to implementing the "service model of the week." Each new change should be introduced with good forethought and be allowed enough time to demonstrate success or failure. Failure should be something to learn from so that mistakes are not repeated. Dwelling on it is punishing and freezes an organization or a family. We should move on from a bad experience and look at other possibilities.

Another reason there is entrenchment in the disability field is bureaucracy and perpetual organizational planning. Bob Dylan said it best: "You don't need a weatherman to know which way the wind blows."[77] Overdone bureaucratic study is the surest way of killing innovation. I can't tell you how much public money I have observed being wasted on researching what was already pretty well-established, or on "needs assessments" and "long-range plans" that ultimately collect dust on a shelf somewhere.

Further, the service system's view of quality has grown out of the "management by objectives" mindset and is locked into the idea that measurement completely controls accountability. While certain kinds of accomplishments can relate well to this approach, there is an over-reliance in the disability field on minimum standards, objectives and data, and excessive documentation and certification. Quality of life is not easily quantified, nor do minimum standards ensure its presence.

I certainly don't think we should spend any more money and time on needs assessments. Instead, we should create an atmosphere of encouragement and innovation through brainstorming and trial runs of different ideas. I think anyone can tell you what people with disabilities need. People with disabilities have been trying to tell us for a long time.

People need a decent home and a good job that pays decent wages.

They need to live in a nice community surrounded by their friends and neighbors, and when appropriate, family.

Their homes should be places where they can pursue those things they want or need or that make them happy, whether these things are spiritual, artistic, financial, athletic, recreational, or medical, or fall into some other domain.

People with disabilities need to be seen as people first. They need to be valued for whatever gifts they have. Many will need the support of a publicly funded system, but not one that will segregate them or place them in an environment over which they have little or no control.

In other words, what is true for people with disabilities is true for all of us.

π—0

C O N C L U S I O N

Unlocking the
Deviancy Dynamic

"Outside the street's on fire in a real death waltz
Between what's flesh and what's fantasy
And the poets down here don't write nothing at all
They just stand back and let it all be"
— Bruce Springsteen

Any other minority group subjected to the kinds of living conditions, poverty, and even exploitation that people with severe disabilities have faced would elicit mass indignation. But so far, a demand for social justice from citizens with disabilities and other advocates has not been able to capture the imagination of middle America.

For too many people in America, people with disabilities are like something unexpected they encounter while out living life. There is mild curiosity, but ultimately there is largely indifference. This is despite the fact that we have constructed our own Berlin wall to keep people with disabilities contained on their side of society.

Even for many of those who serve people with disabilities, there is no indignation or revolt. Righteous anger seems to have been replaced instead by a sense of necessity – the need to care for eternal children who don't know or understand what they are missing. How many times have we all heard it: "He has the mind of a two-year-old."

This is plain wrong. Children with disabilities do not remain children their whole lives. Even if a person's intellectual capacity is limited, he or she still grows into an adult with adult needs. Reading at a two-year-old's level, or having incontinence, for example, do not equate with being two years old. Even emotionally immature adults legally deemed incompetent still must be viewed and treated as adults. This does not mean they should be treated exactly the same as everyone else, but as adults with the same needs and desires as everyone else.

People with disabilities need not live in isolation from the rest of us.

Their lives need not be defined by their disability.

And they should not be subject to programs that segregate them for employment, housing, and recreation, programs that are largely the result of professional convenience.

People with disabilities are much more capable than most people understand, and they should have opportunities to contribute to neighborhoods, workplaces and civic life.

I believe that the core attitude that must change is our belief that we must always focus on trying to "fix" what is wrong with people. While there is nothing wrong per se with working on one's shortcomings, the process can become a minefield for the recipient when there is unequal distribution of power in favor of the ones doing the fixing. We professionals have our expertise, but professionals are far from infallible and can make major mistakes. It was professionals, after all, who built the Titanic.

This approach has led us down a road of labeling, segregations, specialization, facilities, and a readiness requirement to rejoin life that few people with disabilities are reaching.

When I was just a boy in the early sixties, my parents would take me to the neighborhood barbershop. It was called

Cono's. It was there that I first met a person with an intellectual disability. I don't know his real name, but everyone called him "Bobo." Bobo was about thirty years old, and Cono had hired him to sweep up the hair. You could tell Bobo loved his job, and everyone at the barbershop, workers and customers alike, treated him with respect.

This was a time before there were so many specialized facilities designed for people like Bobo, and he didn't seem to miss them at all. Bobo's job is an example of a community accommodating one of its members. The difference is clear between remedying Bobo's inabilities by removing him from his community or figuring out a place and a way in which he could belong in it.

I do not advocate for a return to a time when there were no resources for community support for people with disabilities. But I do think we should spend money much more wisely. The disability field desperately needs to change. But systems don't change dramatically on their own; it is the key people in them who do. In my early years in the field, I thought it would be the experienced disability professionals and researchers who would show the way. Some have done so, but the resulting change has not been nearly enough. While there are very good people among these ranks – some of them close friends of mine trying to make a difference – too many professionals seem more interested in the self-perpetuation of their programs. I think we need to start being more concerned with how many lives we have changed, and not just for the better, but for the best of what is possible.

The people I do want to celebrate are those people with disabilities speaking up, protesting, and lobbying for change. And I want to thank those professionals in the universities and those who provide direct service in the field who are willing to stand up and say the emperor has no clothes, even if it means they put next year's funding at risk.

This book will surely irritate some people. But irritation can produce change. When an irritant becomes trapped in an oyster, the animal senses its presence and begins to coat it, eventually forming a pearl. I hope we will see more pearls created for people with disabilities in my lifetime.

●

This book is my way of apologizing, Raymond, for what I did not do many years ago. I now know I should have made them unlock your room. I should have made them stop giving kids cold showers. I should have stood up to those who made the rules that ultimately wasted so much of your life.

I have learned that there are so many more people like you, Raymond, living lives that are just as locked as you were in your room. Locked from the outside. They are in places and programs that hide them from everyday people. But the keys are for the taking.

We just need to stop accepting what is and start creating what should be.

Photo of Willowbrook from *Christmas in Purgatory* courtesy Center on Human Policy, Syracuse University

ENDNOTES

1   The Developmental Disabilities Assistance and Bill of Rights Act, Title 42, Chapter 144

2   U.S. Department of Health and Human Services, *The Supply of Direct Support Professionals Serving Individuals with Intellectual Disabilities and Other Developmental Disabilities: Report to Congress* (2006). http://aspe.hhs.gov/daltcp/reports/2006/DSPsupply.htm#intro

3   The Developmental Disabilities Assistance and Bill of Rights Act, Title 42, Chapter 144

4   Social Security Administration, *Disabled Beneficiaries Receiving Social Security, SSI, or Both: Annual Statistical Report on the Social Security Disability Insurance Program*, 2004.

5   The Americans with Disabilities Act of 1990, Titles I and V. (Pub. L. 101-336) PL 106-402

6   B. Blatt, *Christmas in Purgatory*, (Syracuse: Human Policy Press, 1974).

7   G. Rivera, *A Personal Crossroad*, August 13, 2004. http://www.geraldo.com/index.php?/archives/18_A_Personal_Crossroad.html

8   D. Davis, W. Fox-Grage, and S. Gehshan, *Deinstitutionalization of Persons with Developmental Disabilities: A Technical Assistance Report for Legislators* (National Council of State Legislators, 2000). http://www.ncsl.org/programs/health/Forum/pub6683.htm

9   D. Braddock, R. Hemp, M. Rizzolo, D. Coulter, L. Haffer, and M. Thompson, *State of the States in Developmental Disabilities* (Washington, DC: American Association on Mental Retardation, 2005).

10 B. Rimland, "Reopen the Institutions? Advocates Reverse Stand as 'Community' Tragedy Unfolds," *Autism Research Review International* 11, no. 1 (1997). http://www.autismwebsite.com/ari/newsletter/reopen.htm

11 Garrity v. Gallen, 522F. Supp. 171 (DNH 1981)

12 D. Eisenhower, *Farewell Radio and Television Address to the American People*, (January 17, 1961) http://www.presidency.ucsb.edu/mediaplay.php?id=12086&admin=34

13 U.S. Department of Health and Human Services, *The Supply of Direct Support Professionals Serving Individuals with Intellectual Disabilities and Other Developmental Disabilities: Report to Congress* (2006).

214

14 U.S. Senate, Michael B. Enzi, Chairman, Committee on Health, Education, Labor And Pensions, *Opportunities for Too Few? Oversight of Federal Employment Programs for Persons with Disabilities*, Report of the Chairman on Federal Programs for Employment of Persons With Disabilities (October 20, 2005).

15 "Nonprofits Should Set CEO Salary Standards," *The Oregonian, (*Oct. 20, 2005).

16 H. Becker, *Outsiders: Studies in the Sociology of Deviance* (New York: The Free Press, 1963).

17 E. Goffman, *Stigma: Notes on the Management of Spoiled Identity,* (Englewood Cliffs, New Jersey: Prentice-Hall (1963).

18 W. Wolfensburger, *Normalization: The Principle of Normalization in Human Services,* (Toronto: National Institute on Mental Retardation, 1972).

19 D. Davis, W. Fox-Grage, and S. Gehshan, *Deinstitutionalization of Persons with Developmental Disabilities: A Technical Assistance Report for Legislators,* (Washington, DC: National Conference on State Legislatures, undated).

20 Agency for Persons with Disabilities, http://apd.myflorida.com/docs/APD-Sen-Com-C_F-10-18-2005.pdf (2005)

21 *Racial Inequity in Special Education: Executive Summary for Federal Policy Makers (*Boston: The Civil Rights Project, Harvard University, 2002).

22 Fact Sheet: Frequently Asked Questions About Mental Retardation. (undated). Washington, DC: American Association on Mental Retardation. http://www.aamr.org/Policies/mental_retardation.shtml

23 *Diagnostic and Statistical Manual of Mental Disorders, Fourth Edition - Text Revision,* (American Psychiatric Association, 2000).

24 R. Luckasson, S. Borthwick-Duffy, W. Buntinx, D. Coulter, E. Craig, A. Reeve, R. Schalock, M. Snell, D. Spitalnik, S. Spreat, and M. Tassé, *Mental Retardation: Definition, Classification, and Systems of Supports,* 10th Ed. (Washington, DC: American Association on Mental Retardation, 2002).

25 M. Gold, *Try Another Way*, (Champaign, IL: Research Press, 1980).

26 U.S. Department of Labor, Employment Standards Administration Wage and Hour Division, *Fact Sheet #39E: Determining Hourly Commensurate Wages to be Paid Workers with Disabilities under Section 14(c) of the Fair Labor Standards Act*, http://www.dol.gov/esa/regs/compliance/whd/whdfs39e.htm.

27 R. Morgan, D. Ellerd, K. Jensen, and M. Taylor, "A Survey of Community Employment Placements: Where Are Youth and Adults with Disabilities Working?" *Career Development for Exceptional Individuals*, 23, no. 1 (2000).

28 H. Boeltzig, D. Gilmore, and J. Butterworth, *The National Survey of Community Rehabilitation Providers, FY2004-2005 Report 1: Employment Outcomes of People with Developmental Disabilities in Employment* (Research to Practice, Institute for Community Inclusion, 2006)

29 G.T. Bellamy, L. Rhodes, D. Mank, and J. Albin, *Supported Employment: A Community Implementation Guide* (Baltimore: Paul H. Brookes Publishing Co., 1988).

30 S. Murphy, and P. Rogan, *Closing the Shop: Conversion for Sheltered to Integrated Work* (Baltimore: Paul H. Brookes Publishing Co., 1995).

31 J. O'Brien, *Discover Community: Learning from Innovations in Services to People with Mental Retardation,* (Atlanta: Responsive System Associates, 1986).

32 L. Brown, *TASH Connections Express*, The Association for Persons with Severe Handicaps (September/October 2005).

33 A. Donnellan, P. Mirenda, R. Mesaros, and L. Fassbender, "Analyzing the Communicative Functions of Aberrant Behavior," *Journal of the Association for Persons with Severe Handicaps* 9, no. 3 (1984).

34 *NOD Survey of Public Attitudes Toward People with Disabilities* (Washington: The National Organization on Disability, 1991).

35 "Special Education Funding," *Education Issues Policy Update* 10, no. 12, National Association of State Boards of Education, (2002). http://www.nasbe.org/Educational_Issues/Policy_Updates/10_12.html

36 Timmy W. v. Rochester NH School District, United States Court of Appeals. 875 F2nd 954 (1st Cir.), (1989).

37 J. L. Down, *Observations on an Ethnic Classification of Idiots,* London Hospital Reports (1866).

38 B.R. Levy, J. Hausdorff, R. Hencke, and J. Wei, "Reducing Cardiovascular Stress with Positive Self-Stereotypes of Aging," *Journal of Gerontology: Psychological Sciences* 55 (2000).

39 J. Monahan, "Mental Disorder and Violent Behavior," *American Psychologist* 47 (1992).

40 R. Abelson, "Employers Increasingly Face Disability-Based Bias Cases," *New York Times* (November 20, 2001).

41 *Executive Summary: The President's New Freedom Commission on Mental Health: Final Report,* (July, 2003).

42 *Legislative Program Review and Investigations Committee* (State of Connecticut, September 3, 1991).

43 "State Drops Plan for Group Home," *The Concord Monitor* (June 4, 1986).

44 W. Wolfensberger, A Brief Introduction to Social Role Valorization as a High Order Concept for Structuring Human Services (Syracuse: Training Institute, 1991).

45 T. Wakefield, Personal Correspondence, Texas (1991)

46 *Wasted Time At Work Costing Companies Billions*, http://www.salary. com.

47 K. Vonnegut, *Cat's Cradle* (New York: Holt, Rinehart, and Winston 1963).

48 H. Tajfel, Experiments in Intergroup Discrimination, *Scientific American* 223 (1970)

49 J. Nisbet and D. Hagner, "Natural Supports in the Workplace: A Reexamination of Supported Employment," *Journal of the Association for Persons with Severe Handicaps* 13 (1988).

50 J. Kretzmann and J. McKnight, *Building Communities from the Inside Out: A Path Toward Finding and Mobilizing a Community's Assets*, (Evanston, IN: Northwestern University, Institute for Policy Research 1993).

51 *Medicaid's Role for People with Disabilities*, The Kaiser Commission on Medicaid and the Uninsured (2003).

52 Wolf Prado-Steiman v. Bush, 221 F.3d 1266 11th Cir. (2000).

53 M. Schuh and B. Dixon, "Consumer and Family Leadership: The Power to Create Positive Futures," *Part of the Community: Strategies for Including Everyone*, ed. J. Nisbet and D. Hagner (Baltimore: Paul H. Brookes Publishing Co., 2000).

54 D. Braddock, R. Hemp, M. Rizzolo, D. Coulter, L. Haffer, and M. Thompson, *State of the States in Developmental Disabilities* (Washington: American Association on Mental Retardation, 2005).

55 *The National Survey of Community Rehabilitation Providers, FY2002-2003, Report 1: Overview of Services and Provider Characteristics* (Boston: Institute for Community Inclusion, August, 2004).

56 L. Jans, S. Stoddard, and L. Kraus, *Chartbook on Mental Health and Disability in the United States, An InfoUse Report* (Washington: U.S. Department of Education, National Institute on Disability and Rehabilitation Research, 2004).

57 L.E. Marshak, D. Bostick, and L.J. Turton, "Closure Outcomes for Clients with Psychiatric Disabilities Served by the Vocational Rehabilitation System," *Rehabilitation Counseling Bulletin* 33 (1990).

58 B. Black and H. Kase, "Changes in Programs over Two Decades," *Work as Therapy and Rehabilitation for the Mentally Ill*, ed. B.J. Black (New York: Altro Health and Rehabilitative Services, 1986).

59 E. Rogers, W. Anthony, J. Toole, and M. Brown, "Vocational Outcomes Following Psychosocial Rehabilitation: A Longitudinal Study of Three Programs," *Journal of Vocational Rehabilitation* 3 (1991).

60 B. Kirsh, "Work, Workers, and Workplaces: A Qualitative Analysis of Narratives of Mental Health Consumers," *Journal of Rehabilitation* 66, no. 4 (2000).

217

61 M. Ellison, K. Danley, C. Bromberg, and V. Palmer-Erbs, "Longitudinal Outcome of Young Adults Who Participated in a Psychiatric Vocational Rehabilitation Program," *Psychiatric Rehabilitation Journal* 22, no. 4 (1999).
62 M. Henderson and M. Argyle, "Social Support by Four Categories of Work Colleague: Relationships Between Activities, Stress, and Satisfaction, *Journal of Occupational Behavior* 6 (1985).
63 V. Riches and V. Green, "Social Integration in the Workplace for People with Disabilities: An Australian Perspective," *Journal of Vocational Rehabilitation* 19, no. 3, (2003).
64 D. Olson and P. Ferguson, "The Meaning of Relationships in a Supported Employment Site," *Integration at Work: Multiple Methodologies in Research*, ed. D. Sandow and D. Olson (Eugene: University of Oregon, Specialized Training Program, 1991).
65 D. Mank, foreword to *Working Together: Workplace Culture, Supported Employment, and Persons with Disabilities* by D. Hagner and D. DiLeo (Cambridge: Brookline Books, 1993).
66 *Small Business and Self-Employment for People with Disabilities*, U.S. Department of Labor, Office of Disability Employment Policy, http://www.dol.gov/odep/programs/promotin.htm.
67 A.W. Doyel, *No More Job Interviews! Self Employment Strategies for People with Disabilities* (St. Augustine, FL: Training Resource Network, Inc., 2000).
68 D. Braddock, R. Hemp, M. Rizzolo, D. Coulter, L. Haffer, M. Thompson, *State of the States in Developmental Disabilities* (Washington: American Association on Mental Retardation, 2005).
69 A. O'Hara and M. Miller, *Priced Out in 2000: The Crises Continues,* (Consortium for Citizens with Disabilities Housing Task Force, 2001) http://www.c-c-d.org/POin2000.html
70 *Achieving Independence: The Challenge for the 21st Century* (National Council on Disability, 2004) http://www.ncd.gov/newsroom/publications/1996/achieving_2.htm
71 J. Klein and M. Black, *Extending the American Dream: Home Ownership for People with Disabilities* (Durham, NH: University of New Hampshire, Institute on Disability, 1991).
72 D. Metzel, "The Extent of Consumer-Directed Funding by MR/DD State Agencies in Day and Employment Services," *Research to Practice* 5 (Boston: Institute for Community Inclusion, 2001)
73 R. Putnam, *Bowling Alone: The Collapse and Revival of American Community* (New York: Simon and Shuster, 2000).
74 J. Campbell and B. Moyers, *The Power of Myth*, ed. Betty Sue Flowers (New York: Doubleday, 1988).

218

75 A. Condeluci, *Interdependence: The Route to Community*, 2nd ed. (Winter Park, FL: GR Press, 1995).
76 W. Whitman, *Leaves of Grass* (1855).
77 B. Dylan, "Subterranean Homesick Blues," *Bringing It All Back Home*, (Columbia, 1965).

π—0
Q U O T A T I O N S

The quotations I selected to begin each chapter have come from people who have inspired me in my years in the disability field.

Chapter One
Gunnar Dybwad, *Children in Russia's Institutions* (UNICEF Report, 1999)

Chapter Two
Harriet McBryde Johnson, "Unspeakable Conversations," *New York Times*, (February 16, 2003).

Chapter Three
Robert Perske, "The Dignity of Risk," *Normalization: The Principle of Normalization in Human Services*, ed. W. Wolfensburger, (Toronto: National Institute on Mental Retardation, 1972).

Chapter Four
Herb Lovett, *Cognitive Counseling and Persons with Special Needs: Adapting Behavioral Approaches to the Social Context* (New York: Praeger Publishers, 1985).

Chapter Five
Judith Snow, *The Quiet Voice*, http://www.communityworks.info/judithmessage.htm

Chapter Six
John McKnight, *Regenerating Community: The Recovery of a Space for Citizens* (Institute for Policy Research, Distinguished Public Policy Lecture Series, 2003).

Chapter Seven
Lou Brown, *The Stories of Lou Brown* (Bloomington: University of Indiana, The Forum on Education, 2005). This manuscript is contained on Video Disc #2 of *Lou Brown Unplugged: A Lifetime of Experiences Advocating for Individuals With Disabilities, Their Family Members and the Professionals Who Serve Them.*

Chapter Eight
J. O'Brien, *Down Stairs That Are Never Your Own* (Atlanta: Responsive Systems Associates, 1991).

Chapter Nine
Marc Gold, "An End to the Concept of Mental Retardation: Oh, What a Beautiful Morning," *Try Another Way* (Champaign, IL: Research Press, 1980)

Conclusion

Bruce Springsteen, "Jungleland," *Born to Run* (Columbia, Sony BMG Music Entertainment, Inc., 1975). (I was born and raised in central New Jersey. Exit 11. Enough said.)

A B O U T   T H E   A U T H O R

A widely sought-after speaker and consultant, and a well-known advocate for people with disabilities, Dale DiLeo has provided training throughout the United States and in Canada and Europe on community inclusion for people with disabilities. Dale has trained tens of thousands of participants over the past thirty years, serving as the keynote for the European Union of Supported Employment in Oslo, Norway, and presenting again in Barcelona, Spain. He has consulted with state and private agencies, families, universities, and professional associations. He is the past president of the board of the Association for Persons in Supported Employment (APSE), and is the lead author of that organization's highly respected *Ethical Guidelines in Supported Employment*. In 2006, he was named a lifetime founding member of the APSE Emeritus Circle. Dale is also the author of several books in the disability field, including *Enhancing the Lives of Adults with Disabilities*, *Reach for the Dream*, and *Working Together* (co-author). With his wife Dawn Langton, he co-wrote *Get the Marketing Edge, A Job Developer's Toolkit*. He lives with Dawn and their daughter, Letty, in historic St. Augustine, Florida.

π—0
I N T E R V I E W
W I T H   D A L E   D I L E O

Q: Why did you write a book condemning the segregation of people with disabilities at this point in your career?

Dale: I spent the first ten years of my career working in or running facilities that were segregated programs. As my philosophy evolved, and my skills developed along with the disability field, I starting working more with supported employment and supported living, more integrated approaches. This is what I have been doing for the last twenty years of my career. But now, despite overwhelming evidence on the benefits of integration, I believe the disability field is still stuck in an obsolete model that is ineffective, morally wrong, and resisting change. Every day the number of people going into segregated programs far exceeds those in more integrated ones. This book is my attempt to call attention to that fact, and to talk about what is possible.

Q: You compare the disability service system to President Eisenhower's concept of a military industrial complex. Is that a fair comparison?

Dale: As someone who worked from the inside of it, I think it is. Eisenhower rightly warned us of a self-perpetuating focus on maintaining funding, lots of bureaucracy, and results that don't always make it to the people most in need. For all the paperwork, there is little real accountability to the people being served.

Q: Proponents of institutions or workshops and group homes say that people have chosen these options and that they report they are happy there. How do you respond?

Dale: Yes, I know that can be true, but it is an incomplete statement. I remember working to help people move out of an institution, a place most of us would agree was horribly offensive. Yet, there were a number of people who expressed that they did not want to leave, and some of their families also said the same thing. The reason this happens over and over again is that people with disabilities have not had the opportunity to make informed choices. Once people experience community life with the proper supports, in my experience, they nearly always elect to not go back to segregation. When you live in a situation for so long, no matter how inadequate, change can appear threatening. I might add, I think there is a strong argument against the wisdom of using taxpayer dollars to fund a choice that segregates people at all, besides the fact of them having inferior outcomes.

Q: What about people with disabilities who have other friends with disabilities? Why shouldn't they choose to live or work together?

Dale: First of all, loneliness is a compelling issue for anyone who finds him or herself isolated in the community. There is no excuse for those of us in the disability field to let such a thing happen when people live and work in a community. As for friendships between people with disabilities, of course that should be supported and respected. And if people decide they want to live together because they are friends, then I think they should go for it. But that is a far cry from an arbitrary group model where people are placed into slots and rarely select their own roommates. Employment, on the other hand, is something else. Unless some friends who happen to have disabilities want to start a business together, I don't think you can typically pick your co-workers.

Q: What is Raymond's room?

Dale: Raymond's room was a bedroom in a residential facility for children with autism that I worked at early in my career. It was a small, hot, stuffy room where two to four children would sleep. These were the kids that no one trusted or who had misbehaved during the day. Raymond was in there so often it was named after him. It was locked from the outside – those on the inside were powerless. It is my metaphor for much of the disability service system then and now.

Q: You present an argument for people with disabilities living in the community, but you also talk at length and give examples about how the community has not always welcomed people with disabilities. Isn't that a paradox?

Dale: Yes, it is. But a big part of the reason there has been community resistance is the disability service system's tendency to exaggerate people's differences rather than their commonalities. Group homes are different than your neighbor's house in so many ways, so the residents that live there are not seen as your neighbors. There have always been stereotypes of people with disabilities, but our jargon and labels and grouping have contributed to those stereotypes rather than combat them. Another problem is that many people are uncomfortable being with people with disabilities, mostly because they never are with them because the system has segregated people out of their communities. When my daughter goes to school with other children who happen to have disabilities, and plays with them and finds it a natural thing, she will not think twice when someone with a disability works next to her or moves next door. And I have found many people with disabilities benefit tremendously being around others with skills they might not have or interests they haven't considered. And if someone with a disability has a particular hobby or passion, then that becomes a basis for a relationship because they are around a diversity of people, and not just those who share their disability label.

I N D E X

Q

quality 189
questioning assumptions 205

R

Randolph-Sheppard 29
readiness 63
reinforcement restrictions 83
reinforcer 72
relationships 188, 191
residential placements 173
response cost 89
Richmond Times-Dispatch 99
right to privacy 182
Rimland, Bernard 14
Rivera, Geraldo 6

S

satisfaction with services 206
segregation 69
self-determination 179, 188
self-employment 167
self-expression 136
self-fulfilling prophecy 206
self-injurious behavior 72
sheltered workshop 169, 204
  as a safety net 170
  down time in 170
  placement rates from 63
  wages in 57
social capital 192
social connections 137, 192
social glue 129, 194
social identities 130
social isolation 165
social roles 136, 142, 197
special education 37
  funding 93
  minority students 38
Springsteen, Bruce 209
St. Augustine, FL 139

staff, disability services 28
stigma 47, 101
Stigma: Notes on the Management
    of Spoiled Identity 34
sub-minimum wages 58
Supplemental Security Income 184
supported employment 144, 148
supported living 179
  housing and support separated
    181
systematic training 196

T

Tajfel, Henri 130
therapeutic specialists 110, 197
time-out 115
time-out programs 76
Timothy W. vs. Rochester, New
    Hampshire 94
token economy 89
transportation 149

U

unrealistic dreams 122
U.S. Department of Labor 57

V

valued social role 117
values 201
violence in the workplace 99

W

wages 141
waiting lists 35
Willowbrook 4
Wolfensberger, Wolf 34, 117
work 141
work culture 160, 166
work readiness 144